Leader Behavior Theory

Jason White EdD, MS, CCS

PREP Group, LLC
Rockland, ME 04841

Visit us at www.prepgroup.info.

ISBN 978-1-7358944-0-9

Dedication

Thank you to the young scientists in my life who inspire me to
do my best every day
Sara
Emily
Silas

My oldest, Teal
(I'm proud of you)

…and the lovely Mrs. Jessica Finley White, for your support all
these years…

Table of Contents

Preface

The inspiration for studying both behavioral psychologies with leadership came from my own interests and experiences as a leader in the military, state government, and community. Over the years I have seen some incredible leaders fail when taking a new position; likewise, I have seen some accomplish amazing things. Through my studies, I have concluded, that it is the environment that determines leader behavior.

To parrot B.F. Skinner, on page 21 of *About Behaviorism,* published in 1974, I have considered scores of information; books, journal articles, discussions with other scientists, etc., and it would be impossible to credit every single person every single time; likewise, if Skinner is correct, and we truly are the sum of our experiences, then I cannot really claim any idea as my own...could I?

The purpose of this book is to articulate a gap in the research literature relative to leadership studies, to remind scientists of the role behavioral psychology can play in explaining leader behavior, and to emphasize the importance of the environment in shaping and managing leader behavior.

1. Introduction

A Brief History

The concept of leadership has been around since the formal recognition of government and city-states; Mesopotamia began to urbanize around 4000 B.C., with the Sumerians being the first recognized civilization.[1,2] The United States geographical layout and government is modeled after city states.[2]

The study of leadership, as social science, did not emerge until the 1930s.[6] From that time, there have been numerous psychology and social science theories developed to explain leader behavior. Most of these theories rely on constructs verified through correlational calculations of survey data; a research method that was proliferated by Harvard professors of social and behavioral sciences in the 1960s.

Both early and current theories on leader behavior discuss

constructs in terms of behavior terminology; lacking real reference to behavior theory or behaviorism and its subfields. It seems like a tremendous failure on the part of research scientists working in the field of leadership studies to miss or discount such a prominent theory in psychology that has a time-proven record of explaining behavior.

Psychology was thought to be a science of consciousness until John Watson published his 1913 paper, Psychology as the Behaviorist Views It, aimed at shifting the study of consciousness to the study of observable behavior. Watson was intrigued by Ivan Pavlov, a Russian physiologist, and his 1901 experiment where he demonstrated that autonomic responses in dogs could be brought under stimulus control. Watson replicated Pavlov's study in 1920, Conditioned Emotional Reactions, also known as 'The Little Albert Study', demonstrating classical and operant conditioning in humans. Probably one of the greatest contributions resulting from Watson's 1920 study was the demonstration of the transitive properties of stimuli or generalization. Interestingly, if compared to Jean Piaget's stage theory on cognitive development, in terms of assimilation and accommodation, it could be argued that Piaget was really discussing transitive properties of stimuli through the use of constructs.[8] In my opinion, this is where the real problem in research lies, for both psychology and leadership studies. Constructs, even when they correctly explain a phenomenon, are not based on cold hard evidence, such as those in behavior theory. David Elkind, a prominent child psychologist, remarked that he was teasing Piaget, and stated, "Why do you use assimilation and accommodation? In America, we always use stimulus and response." To this, Piaget reportedly stated that the constructs were used to help explain cognitive processes.[5]

After this shift in psychology, Watson became known as the father of behaviorism.[2,7] He studied animal behavior for 12

7

years prior to publishing his hallmark paper in 1913; however, it seems he was not able to show how his animal studies on behavior related to human behavior as well as some of his successors did with their animal studies. B.F. Skinner was able to elaborate on the subject of behaviorism in his book published in 1953, titled: *Science and Human Behavior*, ultimately linking the science of behavior to Charles Darwin's concept of natural selection and adaptation, which included Watson's ideas on behavior.[3,4] Skinner stated the history of behavior likely started when a molecule came to be and was able to reproduce itself, and later elaborated that behavior developed from sets of functions facilitating interaction between an organism and its environment.[9] The history of behavior can be theorized to have been occurring when a molecule was able to reproduce itself to survive in environmental conditions.[9]

Behavioral Psychology and Leader Behavior Timeline

The following timeline should demonstrate the simultaneous evolution of the scientific method, behavioral psychology, and leadership studies (not all-inclusive):

2200 BC-Chinese Xia (Hsia) Dynasty Emperor evaluated public officials every three years using a performance evaluation designed by the Dynasty.

1115 BC-Chinese Chan Dynasty evaluated citizens for civil service.

175 BC-Claudius Galenus (Galen) developed methodologies to demonstrate intelligence is a brain activity and not a heart activity.

384-322 BC-Aristotle, an ancient Greek philosopher, noted when two phenomena occur in close temporal proximity enough times, one, by itself, may generate, as an example, emotion, a mental picture, or response, that the other event or stimulus might by itself or together with a different stimulus.

200-Dark Ages-The progression of scientific thinking was stymied; religion, faith, superstition, and demonology became prominent instead.

313-Christianity became recognized by the Roman Empire, which made medical practice the responsibility of the church.

1550-The study of Philosophy began to gain attention. Johann Weyer, a German physician, noted mental illness might be the cause of bizarre behavior and not witchcraft.

1600s (Early)-French philosopher Rene Descartes noted the influence the environment had on behavior; however, he argued that it was not entirely responsible for influencing behavior.

1600s (Late)-British philosopher, John Locke, noted that people start collecting behavior shaping experience from the time they are born.

1600s (Late)-British philosopher, Thomas Hobbes, noted that behavior was the result of either pleasure or avoidance of pain.

1824-Auguste Comte, was a 'positivist' and French philosopher who argued that for humans to change in positive ways, they must obtain knowledge. Human knowledge is reached when empirical data, reason, and the development of scientific laws are used to explain phenomena.

1840-Thomas Carlyle published, *On Heroes, Hero Worship, and the Heroic in History*, which popularized the concept of the great man theory; a theory that stated leaders are born and not developed.

1859-Charles Darwin published *On the Origin of Species*, which introduced the concept of natural selection.

1860-Herbert Spencer expressed opposition to the great man theory by stating that **leaders are a product of the environment**. Unfortunately, instead, the great man theory was the most prominent theory for about the next 100 years.

1873-William Wundt published his book, *Principles of Physiological Psychology*, which discussed the scientific study of behavior as it relates to the environment.

1879 -Wilhelm Wundt established the first psychology lab with an emphasis on systematic methodologies to observe and analyze themes as people described their mental processes. This introspective type of psychology was referred to as structuralism.

1883-G. Stanley Hall, who was a student of Wundt, established the first experimental psychology lab, in the United States, at Johns Hopkins University.

1885-Herman Ebbinghaus published a paper on memory using methodologies for data collection and experimentation by manipulating variables in the environment; a methodology that set the foundation for the development of the scientific method in psychology.

1886-Joseph Jastrow received the first doctorate in psychology; he was a student of G. Stanley Hall at Johns Hopkins University.

1887-G. Stanley Hall established the *American Journal of Psychology*.

1888-James McKeen Cattell, a student of Wundt, became the first professor of psychology and taught at the University of Pennsylvania and Columbia.

1890-William James published *Principles of Psychology*, which took more than 12 years to complete. He noted the importance the environment had on consciousness and behavior. This brand of psychology became known as functionalism.

1892-G. Stanley Hall founded the American Psychological Association; he served as its first president.

1896-Lighter Witmer opened the first-ever psychological clinic to serve patients.

1900-Sigman Freud published some of the most famous components of his theory in *The Interpretation of Dreams*. Psychoanalysis as a field of psychology is established.

1901-Ivan Pavlov, a Russian physiologist, conducted his experiment where he demonstrated that autonomic responses in dogs could be brought under stimulus control. This phenomenon became known as 'classical conditioning'.

1904-Mary Calkins was elected as the first female president of the APA. She studied with William James at Harvard University; however, she was not awarded her doctorate because of her gender.

1905-Alfred Binet developed the first IQ test.

1905-Edward Thorndike published his study, known as the 'Puzzle Box'; he set up an escape contingency where a cat was placed in a box and was required to push a lever to escape. The escape was thought to be the reinforcer to pushing the lever. He demonstrated that when all variables are held constant in a response contingency, the contingency would be predictive of behavior; also known as the 'Law of Effect'.

1913-John B. Watson published his groundbreaking paper, Psychology as the Behaviorist Views It, emphasizing the that only observable behavior should be measured. He had a tremendous influence on psychology and learning theory.

1917-G. Stanley Hall established the Journal of Applied Psychology.

1920-Jean Piaget began to publish his theories on cognitive development.

1920-John B. Watson and Rosalie Reynor published their paper, Conditioned emotional reactions, also known as the 'Little Albert Study', where he demonstrated that like stimuli can have transitive properties (one stimulus can be generalized to another when it is similar); also referred to as 'generalization'.

1921-Hermann Rorschach developed a personality test based on interpretations of inkblots.

1922-Sigmond Freud published his book titled, *A General Introduction to Psychoanalysis.*

1929-B. F. Skinner enrolled in a graduate program at Harvard University to study psychology.

1930s-The study of leadership, as a social science began.

1935-Kurt Koffla published *Principles of Gestalt Psychology.*

1938-B. F. Skinner published *The Behavior of Organisms*; a book about operant conditioning (behavior that operates on the environment).

1943-Abraham Maslow published his paper, A Theory of Human Motivation, which discussed a hierarchy of human needs.

1943-Clark Hull introduced Drive-Reduction Theory, based on the concept of homeostasis.

1945-B. F. Skinner published, On the operational analysis of terms in the journal: *The Behavioral and Brain Sciences.*

1947-B. F. Skinner began lectures on William James studies, regarding verbal behavior, at Harvard.

1948-B. F. Skinner published *Walden Two*, a fictional book about a utopian society that is entirely maintain by contingencies. These types of societies still exist today.

1950-Fred Keller and William Schoenfeld published, *Principles of Psychology*; a textbook with an emphasis on observable behavior. It was a major contribution to behavioral psychology.

1951-John Bowlby introduced attachment theory through the World Health Organization.

1952-Jean Piaget published his book, *The Origins of Intelligence in Children*, which discussed his stage theory on cognitive development.

1953-Ogden Lindsley and B. F. Skinner built a research lab specifically designed to observe behavior.

1953-B. F. Skinner published *Science and Human Behavior*.

1954-Abraham Maslow published *Motivation and Personality*, which focused on the humanistic perspective with an emphasis on choice and life goals. It rejected scientific objectivity to the evaluation of behavior, and instead, focused on the mind and conscious experience.

1956-Nathin Azrin published the first experimental work on punishment.

1957-C. B. Ferester and B. F. Skinner published Schedules of Reinforcement, a record of various experimental analysis of contingencies found in animals.

1957-B. F. Skinner published *Verbal Behavior*.

1957-*Journal of the Experimental Analysis of Behavior* established.

1958-Harry Harlow experimented with monkeys to demonstrate that meeting basic needs is not enough to build attachment. Margaret Ainsworth latter confirmed this in human beings, in what became known as the 'Strange Situation Experiment'.

1958-The *Journal of Experimental Analysis of Behavior* was established.

1958-Noam Chomsky published his criticism of Skinner's verbal behavior.

1960-Murray Sidman published *Tactics in Scientific Research*.

1961-James F. Holland and B. F. Skinner published *The Analysis of Behavior*.

1961-Teodoro Ayllon and Nathan Azrin introduced the 'Token Economy' at Anna State Hospital in Illinois.

1961-Albert Bandura, Dorothea Ross, and Sheila Ross published their study, Transmission of aggression through imitation of aggressive models, also known as the 'BoBo Doll Study', which catalyzed the development of the social learning theory.

1963-Jack Michael Published *Laboratory Studies in Operant Behavior.*

1964-Fred Fielder introduced contingency theory; a theory of personality that is predictive of leader effectiveness.

1964-Victor Vroom introduced expectancy theory; a theory that looks at motivation through the individual's sum of experiences and effort, reward, and values.

1965-Ted Ayllon and Nate Azrin successfully implemented the first token economy treatment program at Anna State Hospital in Illinois. This community is still active today.

1967-Kathleen Kincaid founded Twin Oaks in Louisa, Virginia; a utopian society based on Skinner's *Waldon Two.*

1968-Journal of Applied Behavior Analysis was founded; Donald Baer, Montrose Wolf, and Todd Risley published, as the opening article, Some Current Dimensions of Applied Behavior Analysis, which became a seminal article laying the foundation for research in the journal and the field.

1968-B. F. Skinner was awarded the National Medal of Science.

1969-Paul Hersey and Ken Blanchard introduced situational leadership theory, as a leadership model that alternates between leadership styles based on situation.

1969-University of Florida offered the first doctoral program in behavior analysis.

1970-Richard Herrnstein published On the Law of Effect, to review Edward Thorndike's experiments in behavior, resulting in what is known as the 'Matching Law', which states that the reinforcer must be commensurate to the behavior to be considered an effective reinforcer.

1971-B. F. Skinner published *Beyond Freedom and Dignity*, which claimed there was no such thing as free will.

1976-Richard Dawkins published *The Selfish Gene*, which looked at human behavior through a biological and evolutionary view.

1977-Aubrey Daniels established the Journal of Organizational Behavior Management, and published, as a seminal editorial, citing Baer et al.'s (1968) direction to the field of applied behavior analysis, as direction to the field of organizational behavior management with the caveat that organizational behavior management is useful for managers addressing problems in the organizational setting.

1978-Aubrey Daniels started his company, Aubrey Daniels & Associates, to consult on workplace problems using applied behavior analysis.

1985-Aubrey Daniels published his book, *Bringing Out the Best in People*.

1987-The B. F. Skinner Foundation was established.

1987- Donald Baer et al., updated their original article from 1968, titled, Some still current dimensions of applied behavior analysis.

1993-Nancy Neef was elected as the first female editor of the Journal of Applied Behavior Analysis.

1998-Behavior Analyst Certification Board (BCBA) was established.

2007-John Cooper, Timothy Heron and William Heward published a textbook titled, *Applied Behavior Analysis (2 ed.)*, which became the study guide for the BCBA certification.

2007-Aubrey Daniels and James Daniels published, *Measure of a Leader*, which largely discusses leadership in terms of behavior analysis.

2020-Jason White published his book, *Leader Behavior Theory*, which combines leadership theory with applied behavior analysis.

Chapter One References

[1]Adams, L. S. (2002). *Art across time.* New York, NY: McGraw-Hill Companies.

[2]American Psychological Association. (2007). *APA dictionary of psychology.* Washington, DC: American Psychological Association.

[3]Catania, A. C. (2003). B. F. Skinner's science and human behavior: Its antecedents and its consequences. *Journal of the Experimental Analysis of Behavior,* 80 (3), 313-320.

[4]Darwin, C. (1859). *On the origin of species by means of natural selection.* London, UK: John Murray.

[5]Elkind, D. (2016). *On Jean Piaget.* Retrieved from https://www.youtube.com/watch?v=lozqMoEvCTI

[6]House, R. J., & Aditya, R. N. (1997). The social scientific study of leadership: Quo vadis? *Journal of Management,* 23 (3), 409-473.

[7]Luthans, F. (2015). Fred Luthans: The anatomy of a 50-year academic career. *University of Nebraska-Lincoln.* Retrieved on July 26, 2015 from https://www.youtube.com/watch?v=eVd53xKOi2I.

[8]Piaget, J. P. (1952). *The origins of intelligence in children.* International Universities Press, New York.

[9]Skinner, B. F. (1981). Selection by consequences. *Science,* 213, 501-504.

[10]Watson, J. B. (1913). Psychology as the behaviorist views it. *Psychological Review,* 20, 158-177.

[11]Watson, J. B. & Rayner, R. (1920). Conditioned emotional reactions. *Journal of Experimental Psychology, 3*(1), 1-14.

[12]White, J. (2014). *Journal of a 2nd lieutenant in Iraq with the 133rd battalion.* Solon, ME: Polar Bear and Company.

2. Key Leadership Theories

Introduction

Early and current leadership theories provide the foundation to conduct research in the leadership studies field and to provide for more updated models to inform practice. Many of the leadership theories still have value and can be a great guide for leaders as they practice; likewise, many of the leadership theories are incredibly complex, and though they may be of excellent value to the scholar, they offer very little assistance to the practicing leader. An effective leader will be one that can adapt to a multitude of different environments.

Trait Theories of Leadership

Leader traits are variables that contribute to effective leadership. Research has focused on predictive relationships between personality types and found that personality traits were predictive of leader behavior.

The idea that people are born with leadership traits has dated back approximately 2,000 years when the concept was expressed in writings by Heraclitus, a pre-Socratic Greek philosopher. Even today, there is a belief that people are born with certain traits that are predictive of how well they will do as leaders as exemplified in Colin Powell's book, *It Worked for Me: In Life and Leadership*, published in 2012, where he remarked that leaders are born with certain traits that increase the probability that they will become leaders.

In early research and leader theory development, the trait theory model, of leaders having innate abilities to lead, was referred to as the 'great man theory', which later morphed into charismatic leadership, a model that preserved the idea that leaders are born with particular traits.[30]

Many social scientists have embraced trait theory and have looked at ways to measure personality traits; for example, measurements of personality traits of manager behavior using 360 measurements. The 360-measurement term indicates the measurements were multi-inventory or multi-assessment based.[7] The traits commonly evaluated are what has been called the 'big five' leadership traits, which are extraversion, emotional stability, agreeableness, conscientiousness, and openness.[7] Other assessments commonly used are self-assessments and external assessments or assessments completed by subordinates and peers. Researchers have found that self-assessments were the strongest predictor of leader behavior; however, it should be noted there may be a bias that cannot be controlled for. It is common for leadership measures to be focused on the performance of the leader's immediate followers and in the form of survey measures.[71] Current research[7] shows that the best evaluation to predict leader behavior comes from external assessments and from subordinates; evaluations completed by supervisors of managers tend to be the weakest predictors of leader behavior. Of the big five, openness, conscientiousness, and agreeableness dimensions are the most closely related to leader behavior, and agreeableness and conscientiousness are noted as being important in predicting ethical behavior.[7]

Gender has been thought of as being a variable related to the effectiveness of influencing others in groups and in work settings; however, studies on leadership and influence that discuss gender note gender is not a variable regarding the effectiveness of influencing others or effectively leading others, in groups and in work settings.[18,30,45,50,75] The implication, for the purposes of this book, is that gender is not a variable that has moderating or impeding effects on leader behavior.

Effectively influencing and leading others depends on how the leader identifies with that particular group, according to S. Alexander Haslam, Stephen Reicher, and Michael Platow, as noted in their book, *The new psychology of leadership: Identity, influence, and power*, published in 2011. They argued that leaders who identify themselves in the first person, such as using 'I' or 'me', are less effective than those who identify themselves in the second person, such as using 'we' or 'us'. In 2006, Reicher and Haslam built on Philip Zimbardo's Stanford Prison Experiment and conducted an experiment where they took a group of adult males and randomly divided them into two groups, prison guards and inmates, in a simulated prison setting. There was not a designated leader among the guards, and no one present as having been thought to have leadership skills. In the prisoner group, there were two individuals thought to have leadership skills. The inmates wanted to address issues individually until they were organized by one of the leader prisoners. Reicher and Haslam were attempting to show that the leader had greater influence with those who could identify with the leader.

Subsequent research has shown leader identity predicts leader behavior and effectiveness.[35] Behaviors that have been looked at were transformational behaviors and abusive behaviors. Identity can be defined as the view of self in relation to others with leader identity being broken down into three levels: collective identity, relational identity, and individual identity. These components, when compared against daily leader behaviors: transformational behavior, consideration behavior, and abusive behavior, using survey data, have shown that leaders who were individually oriented tend to also have an increased probability of engaging in abusive behavior. Other findings have shown that leader relational identity paired with consideration behavior was not predictive of leader effectiveness. This finding seems to contradict previous research in this area of studies.[74] In addition, it should be noted that leader identity and behavior could change from day to day. The totality of research suggests leader identity is not the only variable influencing leader behavior, and that antecedents to behavior can change.

The skills approach to leadership theory is very similar to the trait theory of leadership, which focuses on skills leaders must have to be successful.[49] In this portion of the theory, there are three primary skills: technical (hands-on experience), human (communication and working effectively with others), and conceptual (understanding abstract ideas). Additionally, there are theories that might serve the field of study better if they were

24

combined. D. Scott Derue, Jennifer Nahrgang, Ned Wellman, and Stephen Humphrey[18] attempted to develop what they called 'integrative trait-behavioral model'. Derue, et al. conducted a meta-analysis of meta-analyses to examine leader traits (such as gender, intelligence, and personality) and behaviors (such as transformational-transactional) regarding four criteria (leader effectiveness, group performance, follower job satisfaction, and satisfaction with the leader). What they found, in their meta-analysis of 79 meta-analyses from online databases such as *PsychINFO* (1887-2008) and *Web of Science ISI* (1970-2008), using descriptors such as: leader, leadership, manager; with: meta-analysis and or quantitative research, was that leader behaviors are more predictive of leader effectiveness than leader traits.

The literature shows that research on trait and skills leadership theories do not demonstrate how trait and skill types are related to leader behavior and effectiveness in different environments; traits themselves are not easily defined or observable.[77]

Contingency and Situational Theories of Leadership

Contingency theory models focus on leader effectiveness based on leader styles and situations.[8,22,23,24,49,56] Contingency theory, as introduced by Fred Fielder in 1964, is a theory of personality that is predictive of leader effectiveness.[23,56] The theory is supported by a prodigious amount of research and has been subjected to empirical scrutiny over the years.[44,48,49] Contingency theory, as introduced by Fielder, has three components: leader-member relations, task structure, and position; depending on how they assist in leader effectiveness, are referred to as situational favorableness.[56] Fiedler stated that leader-member relations are the most important dimension, of the three, and position of power is the least important.[22] This is because leaders with weak positions of power can still be effective leaders if they have good relations. According to Fielder, leaders who are task-oriented perform better in very favorable and unfavorable situations than leaders who are relationship-oriented, who do better in moderately favorable situations; however, when leader training and experience are applied, the task-oriented leader typically becomes less effective, while the relationship-oriented leader becomes more effective.[24]

Some criticisms of the contingency and situational leadership theory are that this model is not always replicable, and that other research studies have not been supportive of the model.[23,56] Regardless, there is enough research supporting the predictive property of the theory. Lastly, S. Alexander Haslam, Stephen Reicher, and Michael Platow stated, in their book, when discussing contingency theory, leaders who describe their history of leader success, often describe contingencies; meaning that leaders are not born leaders, but instead are leaders because of circumstances.

Attempts to improve Fielder's model have led to alternate models.[41] The United States Army, for example, uses a contingency based model of leadership, though not giving it any particular name, and uses styles that are: directing style, participating style, and delegating style. The United States Army has noted that each style will depend on the situation; the effective leader will be one who can alternate styles.[17] Situational leadership styles allow leadership style adjustments based on the situation; Paul Hersey, one of the developers of situational leadership theory, stated that there are four styles under situational leadership: telling, selling, participating, and delegating.[31] The idea of situational leadership theory was originally developed in 1969 and the fact that the theory has been around for many years seems to give it some credibility. Some researchers have remarked that it is relatively easy to use, while others have argued that it is difficult, but effective. Another argument might be that its credibility, as a theory, is damaged based on the changes to the theory over time (this will never be the case with leader theory based in applied behavior analysis, because it is based on the scientific method and analysis of empirical data, and has a history of well-established principles as discussed in later chapters).

Another leadership model related to contingency theory is transactional leadership; which is a theory that notes transactional leadership as being an exchange. The exchange is one where followers exchange their commitment to a leader, who in turn exchanges leadership or representation to assist followers to complete a task. This theory contrasts with transformational leadership, which is a leadership model that focuses on improving organizations and performance and focuses on organizational change.[48,59] It has been noted in leadership literature that transactional and transformational leadership have derivatives of behaviorism.[18]

Follower Theories of Leadership

Leadership models, to include behavioral leadership models, that fit under cognitive theories of leadership, can be considered to be mental models of leadership, where leaders are effective because they have valid and effective ways of working through complex situations and not because of greater knowledge and experience.[36] Researchers indicate that it is an ability to learn new information and application of new information to the

27

challenges while leading, that make leaders successful. The leader's ability to change mental models that also make them successful has been thought to have been shaped from transformative learning; being able to learn new models and skills through leadership training, seminars, courses, etc. According to Homer Johnson, who published a study on mental models of leadership, most executive leaders find their largest learning experience was through some failure. Johnson seemed to interpret this as a challenge to mental models or being forced to change mental models.[36]

Homer Johnson noted that to change mental models, reflection and challenging experiences are key as a leader works their way up the ladder. He stated that these challenges can be in various forms, such as a change in task, position, and increased responsibilities. Johnson also noted that leaders who develop healthy coping skills are more effective leaders. Subsequent research supported the argument made here, that significant events assist in learning.[67]

The literature on follower theories of leadership demonstrates that follower behavior may influence the leader and leader efficacy or leader confidence.[72] Self-efficacy is being able to reflect on the self, in some way, to change behavior.[2] Survey data has been used to show when follower behavior was positive, the leader was more confident, and when the follower behavior was negative, the leader was less confident.[72] Additionally, when follower behavior was positive, there was not a difference in respondent behavior among males and females. When respondent behavior was negative, male leader confidence was less affected. It should be reiterated that research in this arena found gender did not have an influence on leadership ability.

Research into the relationship between leader behavior and their subordinates' expectations of their job show four leader behaviors: directive, supportive, participative, and achievement oriented. Sikandar Hayat Malik published a journal article where he demonstrated that gender, age, education, and experience were not influential in job expectancies; however, he showed supervisors' job expectancies are most often different than that of their leaders.[45] Leader behavior impacts job expectancies of subordinates. Supportive leader behavior has been shown to be effective, which is contradictory to some research in the field, where participative leader behavior is thought to be the most effective.[45]

Self-regulation theory is a theory that states tension in groups is what makes groups function. Specific variables identified in this theory are the nature of group inputs such as whether the group is open or closed; open meaning that there are outside inputs and closed meaning that inputs generated within the group. In this theory, there are three main components to group regulation: Self-awareness, clear standards and goals, and ability and willingness to make changes. The leader, as a manager of these three components, can affect the success of the group. Failure is often natural and that the leader is the corrective action.[52]

A theory that considers leadership as it relates to behavior and where people are located in a group is referred to as organizational citizenship behavior or OCB. The term, OCB, encompasses membership in small groups where the small group is also a member of a larger organization. In their research, Tal Yaffe and Ronit Kark found that worthiness, is very valuable in being effective, and that the group would need to believe that the leader would be able to pull the group forward, and vice versa (that the leader needs to believe that the group is also worthy).[75] Yaffe and Kark conducted a large study to support their finding. They studied a large Israeli communication organization, with 67

29

work units or teams from three separate departments; a service department consisting of 37 teams, a technical department consisting of 21 teams, and a sales department consisting of 9 teams. They surveyed members and leaders using various surveys, appropriate to group membership as a leader, manager, and member containing seven-point scales ranging from 1=strongly disagree to 7=strongly agree or very typical. These surveys were sent to all the 683 employees. Data collected are on variables such as gender and tenure. The results were that when specific conditions are met, both direct leaders and indirect leaders can affect groups. Also, exemplary leadership is effective in group performance. The most important finding, as discussed by Yaffe and Kark, was that leaders who lead by example and set personal standards of OCB are more effective than leaders who do not. The variable labeled as role model was the second strongest positively correlated to the variable labeled as leader OCB with a coefficient of .40 at p>.01 (group tenure and leader OCB were the highest correlated at .44).

A leader's profile is essential in influencing others; effective leaders are those that can levy resources and represent their followers. Often, the leader is engaged in politics to navigate networks for these resources. According to B. Parker Ellen, who published an article in the *Journal of Organizational Behavior* titled, Considering the positive possibilities of leader political behavior, positive outcomes of leaders is to acquire resources, provide advancement and development opportunities, and restore justice when needed. Ellen[21] noted that effective leaders are ones who have a wide network who use that network to influence followers by assigning high profile tasks with prominent organizational leaders, such as serving on internal workgroups and committees. Ellen, citing his own research, noted that politicking in organizations, as a leader, is essential for supporting followers.

Some of the most prominent researchers in leadership studies are Malcolm Higgs and Deborah Rowland. In their 2011 qualitative study that consisted of interviews of upper-echelon leaders from 33 organizations across the UK, such as non-governmental organizations, volunteer organizations, and charity organizations, they found that 'leader-centric' behavior or leader behavior where the leader put themselves as the focal point for change negatively impacted the change efforts.[33] They found that leaders who exhibit behaviors that are facilitating and engaging are more successful.

Some of the more advanced leadership theories, such as transformational leadership and leader-member exchange or LMX, make it very clear that leaders affect the behavior of others who may not otherwise act on their own.[46] The importance of rapport building with followers is a central component of LMX; followers are followers because they need something from leaders, and leaders would not be leaders unless there were followers. The focus of LMX research has shifted from the behavioral three-term contingency (antecedents, behavior, and consequences) and has failed to consider the environment.[4]

Behavioral Theories of Leadership

Behavior analysis encompasses three subfields: Behaviorism is the subfield of behavior analysis and is the philosophy of the field; experimental analysis is the subfield that is the research component of the field, and applied behavior analysis is the subfield that focuses on the applicability of research findings.[25] Behavior is the activity of a living organism.[16] The main components of behavior theory are antecedents, behavior or response, and consequences or reinforcement; contingencies to maintain or diminish behavior.[14,41,44,62] Behavior theory focuses on behavior in relation to the environment.[14,61,62,63,64]

Much of the research, regarding reinforcement contingencies, is focused on children and teachers. Research has shown that teacher behavior can produce and remove problem behavior in students and supports the 'catch 'em being good' phrase that many parents are often taught.[68] Interestingly, undesirable behavior can also be maintained by a disapproving response.[68] The best scenario, as found in research, is that children's behavior is affected when the teacher is being positive, and when the positive behavior of children is being reinforced.[69]

An interesting study, by Joseph Lalli, Diane Browder, F. Charles Mace, & D. K. Brown, studied the responses of a severely intellectually disabled girl, then diagnosed as severely mentally retarded, given various response contingencies. In the study, Lalli et al. required teachers to conduct a scatter plot analysis over a five-day period, at thirty-minute intervals. The three categories of measurement were: zero incidents, low occurrences (1-10 target behaviors occurring per 30 minutes), and high occurrence times (greater than 10 target behaviors occurring per 30-minute period). After Lalli et al. had identified a response class hierarchy; they applied an escape contingency to each of the topographies while placing the other two responses on extinction. What they demonstrated was that when applied to the last response in the hierarchy, the other responses were observed in order (screams, aggression, and self-injury). When the contingencies were applied to earlier topographies in the hierarchy, subsequent ones did not appear.[38]

Research studies on behavior show, if results are generalizable, that leaders of groups can influence behavior in the form of contingencies and that behavior in typographies will occur in order; in essence, if the contingency is not changed, the leader should expect the same behavior to occur. Richard Herrnstein raised an important consideration with his development of the matching law, which basically stated for a behavior to occur, and keep occurring, at least until satiation is reached, the amount of reinforcement must be commensurate to the behavior (for example, no one would run a marathon for a pizza, the behavior of running a marathon is not reinforced by the pizza).[32] In essence, the principles of behavior theory, specifically applied behavior analysis, can be used by leaders to manage subordinate leader and employee behavior through organizing contingencies in the environment.[41,42,43,44]

Social learning theory is a theory that was born out of behavior theory and is a behavior theory that uses behavior conditioning principles.[41, 42][65,75] Social learning theory can be traced back to Albert Bandura, Dorothea Ross, and Sheila Ross's 1961 study, where they demonstrated that aggressive reaction in children are heightened after exposure to filmed aggression toward a bobo doll (a punching doll of Bobo the Clown that could be purchased as a toy at the time of the study).[5] When the children who viewed the video, were denied preferred toys, and taken to a room that contained the bobo doll, they aggressed toward the doll, even yelling aggressive phrases heard in the video. Since that study, a plethora of studies have been published, demonstrating the effectiveness of modeling in various forms. Attitudes can be developed through modeling, or imitating behavior.[26] Modeling responsible behavior as well as discouraging irresponsible behavior is effective; modeling good health can influence subordinates to live healthy, reduce sick time, and improve leader and follower effectiveness.[51,65, 73] Likewise, leader stress and well-

33

being have been shown to be associated with employee stress and well-being.[60]

There are several types of models that have evolved from original modeling concepts, such as self-modeling and self-efficacy. Self-modeling and self-efficacy are positive behavioral changes through continuous self or video observations of oneself performing a specific behavior.[37] Self-modeling and self-efficacy have been shown to be least restrictive, and not invasive in any way.[13] In addition, behaviors resulting from video self-modeling applications can be generalized across settings, and equipment used in videotaping is relatively unsophisticated.[9,1019,20,40] James Moore and Wayne Fisher, in their research, have also demonstrated that modeling can be an effective way to teach others to also be effective.[47] They conducted a study where they trained observers, in functional behavior analysis procedures, to collect data. Their training consisted of a PowerPoint lecture relating to functional behavioral assessment. In addition, each observer was trained by viewing two videos on interval recording procedures, and then required to demonstrate mastery of the assessment process. The videos contained a small mock classroom with a student demonstrating current target behavior to be recorded. Moore and Fisher demonstrated that video modeling was efficacious in gaining mastery level assessments from trainees when they assessed actual clients after lecture and video modeling. Work-related performance has also been increased with these types of self-modeling and self-efficacy procedures.[66]

During the 1970s, leadership theories stemming from behavioral theory were dominant.[76] Some of these theories were contingency theory, path-goal theory as a product of contingency theory, leader-member exchange theory or LMX, and normative decision-making theory.[41,76] Path-goal theory is under the

34

umbrella of contingency theory.[1] The original idea of exploring the relationship between supervisors and subordinates through a path-goal framework started with Martin Evens, in 1970, after publishing a paper on the subject.[11,34,49] After reading the article, Robert House wanted to expand the theory and contacted Evens regarding it. According to House, Evens reported that he did not develop a theory and encouraged House to do it, which led to House receiving credit for its development.[34] In addition, the theory is partially based on the work of Victor Vroom and his development of expectancy theory, which is a theory of motivation, using valence or reward, expectancy or performance, and instrumentality or belief the reward will be received once the task is completed.[11,12,70]

The path-goal theory was developed to assist leaders in helping followers to identify behaviors that lead to goals, while maintaining consideration of follower needs, situation, and environment, to ensure success and satisfaction of the follower.[49] Leader behavior in conjunction with subordinate characteristics and task characteristics effects the subordinate's motivation to accomplish tasks.[11,49] Leader behaviors are leadership styles; directive or stating explicit instructions, supportive or amicable and approachable, participative or collaborative, and achievement-oriented or establishing high-performance expectations for subordinates' success. Leaders can change their style or behavior depending on the situation.[49] The greatest strength of the path-goal theory is that it is a model designed to assist leaders in clarifying paths to goals and helping subordinates to achieve goals. Some of the theory's weaknesses are that it is complex and broad, there is a lack of research supporting assumptions, and it does not take into consideration how subordinate behavior effects the leader or the leader's behavior.[49]

The leader member exchange theory or LMX, is a theory of leadership that is focused on the relationship between the leader and the subordinate; the dyadic relationship effecting both the leader and the follower.[41,43,49] The theory examines how leaders are connected to the subordinates or groups in terms of being an 'in-group' subordinate (having high-quality relationships), or being an 'out-group' subordinate (having a minimally required relationship that is more formal).[3,49,57] The theory was originally developed as the vertical dyad linkage theory, or VDL, where researchers focused on relationships in a hierarchal sense.[49]

The in-group are typically those subordinates that have high-quality interactions with the leader and tend to do more than what is formally required. The out-group is typically those that have low-quality interactions with the leader and perform at minimum standards. Subordinates with high-quality exchanges tend to be more loyal and contribute to leader performance; whereas, low-quality exchange subordinates tend to receive fewer resources and benefits as a result of their minimum work.[57] The theory makes it very clear that leaders affect the behavior of others who may not otherwise act on their own.[46]

Some of the theory's greatest strengths are that it stresses the importance of leader and subordinate relationships in the accomplishment of tasks and receiving benefits.[49] Some of its weaknesses are that it only examines the relationship either from the leader's perspective or the subordinate's perspective; thus, not really focusing on the dyadic relationship as it purports to. The theory has been added to and simplified, since 1972, often without any rationale.[57,58]

Leadership relationship quality is often studied under the LMX framework.[29] The theory has been one of the most researched theories in leadership studies.[58] Literature around LMX has focused on antecedents and consequences of behavior with a great deal of support for using LMX for within groups and dyadic echelon leader-member exchanges.[4,58] One of the failures of LMX research is the lack of studying relationships in social contexts where leaders and followers likely function.[58]

Transformational leadership theory is the most widely researched leadership theory.[28] It is a large theory that considers leader behavior and the environment. Research into transformational leadership theory support that it can be broken down into two categories: Measurement or how leaders meet transformational criteria, and behavior or looking at why transformational leaders do what they do.[30] Criticisms of transformational leadership are that it lacks an explanation of why certain behaviors are relevant, lacks empirical evidence derived from direct observation on the leader and follower processes, and lacks a clear concept because it is such a diverse and abstract theory.[49,59,77]

Ethical Theories of Leadership

Ethics as part of leader behavior is a dominant theme in research.[15,65] Gunter Stahl and Mary Sully DeLugue published a synthesis of the literature on responsible and irresponsible leader behavior in relation to corporate social responsibility or CSR.[65] This term is the simultaneous consideration of social, environmental, and economic sustainability, sometimes referred to as the triple bottom line. They found ethics was a prominent guiding theme on leadership behavior, discovering two subcategories, 'does good' and 'avoid harm'. Stahl and DeLugue also found that leaders who approach their work through the 'avoid harm' lens are less likely to be irresponsible and the cultural or contextual climate will also determine how leaders and managers will behave. Solid policies and well-defined parameters will lead to responsible leader behavior. When solid policies, rules, and parameters are non-existent, a strong collaborative environment will also lead to responsible leader behavior. Stahl and DeLugue stated that responsible leader behavior is a combination of the individual and the environment that the behavior occurs in. In addition, Stahl and DeLugue noted that that modeling responsible behavior as well as discouraging irresponsible behavior is effective. Stahl and DeLugue named many variables that encourage responsible leader behavior, such as modeling, collaborative decision making, communicating ethical standards, creating and enforcing policies, and training and education initiatives.

Summary

The field of leadership studies and behavioral psychology clearly shows there are a multitude of behaviors effecting leader and follower behavior; however, theories on leadership purporting to be based on behavior, are not based on behavior as science used to explain why leaders behave the way they do. These theories lack consistency across studies and are informed by methods that are either interview or survey-based.[18,39,71,77]

A behavior analysis approach to explain and evaluate leader behavior can fill in some of the gaps where other theories are lacking a best practice procedure such as direct observation, as an example. Behavior analysis encompasses at least 30 years of research that is still used today, specifically functional analysis and inter-observer procedures, which are considered best practices in the field for collecting empirical data.[6] The gap in research for leadership studies is around the true analysis of behavior, as science itself, to explain and discuss variables effecting leader behavior in various environments. Most of the variables discussed by researchers are based on constructs without regard to behavior analysis.[27]

Chapter Two References

[1]Alanazi, T. R., & Raslie, A. M. (2013). Overview of path-goal leadership theory. *Comprehensive Research Journal of Management and Business Studies*, 1 (1), 1-6.

[2]American Psychological Association. (2007). *APA dictionary of psychology*. Washington, DC: American Psychological Association.

[3]Amiri, M. P., Amiri, M. P., & Amiri A. P. (2010). A dynamic model of contingency leadership effectiveness. *Clinical leadership & management review*, 24(2), 1-10.

[4]Avolio, B., Walumbwa, F., & Weber, T. J. (2009). Leadership: Current theories, research, and future directions. *Management Department Faculty Publications*, 37, 420-449.

[5]Bandura, A., Ross, D., & Ross, S. A. (1961). Transmission of aggression through imitation of aggressive models. *Journal of Abnormal and Social Psychology, 63*, 575-582.

[6]Beavers, G. A., Iwata, B. A., & Lerman, D. C. (2013). Thirty years of research on the functional analysis of problem behavior. *Journal of Applied Behavior Analysis*, 46 (1), 1-21.

[7]Bergman, D., Lornudd, C., Sjoberg, L. & Von Thiele Schwarz, U. (2014). Leader personality and 360-degree assessments of leader behavior. *Scandinavian Journal of Psychology*, 55, 389-397.

[8]Bons, P. M., & Fielder, F. E. (1976). Changes in organizational leadership and behavior or relationship and task motivated leaders. *Administrative Science Quarterly*, 21 (3), 453-473.

[9]Buggey, T. (2005) Video self-modeling applications with students with autism spectrum disorder in a small private school setting. *Focus on Autism and Other Developmental Disabilities, 20(1), 52-63.*

[10]Clare, C. K., Jenson, W. R., Kehle, T. J., & Bray, M. A. (2000). Self-modeling as a treatment for increasing on-task behavior. *Psychology in the Schools, 37(6), 517-522.*

[11]Clark, D.R. (2013). *Path-goal leadership theory*. Retrieved November 23, 2014, from http://www.nwlink.com/~donclark/leader/lead_path_goal.html.

[12]Clark, D. R. (2014). *Leadership & human behavior*. Retrieved November 23, 2014, from http://www.nwlink.com/~donclark/leader/leadhb_2.html.

[13]Clark, E., Kehle, T. J., Jenson, W. R., & Beck, D. E. (1992). Evaluation of the parameters of self-modeling interventions. *School Psychology Review, 21(2), 246-254.*

[14]Cooper, J. O., Heron, T. E., & Heward, W. L. (2007). *Applied behavior analysis* (2nd ed.). Upper Saddle River, NJ: Pearson Prentice Hall.

[15]Dadhich, A. & Bhal, K. T. (2008). Ethical leader behavior and leader-member exchange as predictors of subordinate behaviors. *VIKALPA: The Journal for Decision Makers*, 33 (4), 15-25.

[16]Daniels, A. C., & Daniels, J. E. (2005). *Measure of a leader*. Atlanta, GA: Performance Management Publications.

[17]Department of the Army. (2009). *FM 22-100: Military Leadership*. Department of the Army.

[18]Derue, S. D., Nahrgang, J. D., Wellman, N., & Humphrey, S. E. (2011). Trait and behavioral theories of leadership: An integration and meta-analytic test of their relative validity. *Personnel Psychology*, 64, 7-52.

[19]Dowrick, P. W., & Dove, C. (1980) The use of self-modeling to improve the swimming performance of spina bifida children. *Journal of Applied Behavior Analysis, 13,* 51-56.

[20]Dowrick, P. W., & Hood, M. (1981). Comparison of self-modeling and small cash incentives in a sheltered workshop. *Journal of Applied Psychology, 66(3),* 394-397.

[21]Ellen, B. P. (2014). Considering the positive possibilities of leader political behavior. *Journal of Organizational Behavior*, 35, 892-896.

[22]Fielder, F. E. (1965). Engineer the job to fit the manager. *Harvard Business Review*, 43 (5), 115-122.

[23]Fielder, F. E. (1971). Validation and extension of the contingency model of leadership effectiveness: A review of empirical findings. *Psychological Bulletin*, 76 (2), 128-148.

[24]Fielder, F. E. (1972). The effects of leadership training and experience: A contingency model of interpretation. *Administrative Science Quarterly*, 17 (4), 453-470.

[25]Fisher, W. W., Groff, R. A., & Roane, H. S. (2011). Applied behavior analysis: History, philosophy, principles, and basic methods. In W. W. Fisher, C. C. Piazza, & H. S. Roane (Eds.), *Handbook of applied behavior analysis* (pp. 3-13). New York, NY: The Guilford Press.

[26]Fiske, S. T. (2004). *Social Beings*. Danvers, MA: John Wiley & Sons.

[27]Gambrill, E. (2007). Views of evidence-based practice: Social workers' code of ethics and accreditation standards as guides for choice. *Journal of Social Work Education*, 43 (3), 447-462.

[28]Greene, M. (1993). The passions of pluralism: Multiculturalism and the expanding community. *Educational Researcher*, 22(1), 13-18.

[29]Harris, K. J., & Wheeler, A. R., & Kacmar, K. M. (2009). Leader-member exchange and empowerment: Direct and interactive effects on job satisfaction, turnover intentions, and performance. *The Leadership Quarterly*, 20, 371-382.

[30]Haslam, S. A., Reicher, S. D., & Platow, M. P. (2011). *The new psychology of leadership: Identity, influence, and power.* New York, NY: Psychology Press.

[31]Heresy, P. (2014). Hersey-Blanchard situational leadership theory. Retrieved from www.leadership-central.com/situational-leadership-theory.html on May 19, 2014.

[32]Herrnstein R. J. (1970). On the law of effect. *Journal of Experimental Analysis of Behavior*,13,243–266.

[33]Higgs, M. J., & Rowland, D. (2011). What does it take to implement change successfully? A study of behaviors of successful change leaders. *The Journal of Applied Behavioral Science*, 47(3) 309-335.

[34]House, R. J. (1996). Path-goal theory of leadership: Lessons, legacy, and a reformulated theory. *Leadership Quarterly*. 7 (3): 323–352.

[35]Johnson, H. H. (2008). Mental models and transformative learning: The key to leadership development? *Human Resource Development Quarterly,* 1, 85-89.

[36]Johnson, R. E., Venus, M., Lanaj, K., Mao, C., & Chang, C. (2012). Leader identity as an antecedent of the frequency and consistency of transformational, consideration, and abusive leadership behaviors. *Journal of Applied Psychology*, 97(6), 1262-1272.

[37]Kehle, T. J., Owen, S. V., & Cressy, E. T. (1990). The use of self-modeling as an intervention in school psychology: A case study of an elective mute. *School Psychology Review*, 19 (1), 115-121.

[38]Lalli, J. S., Browder, D. M., Mace, F. C., & Brown, D. K. (1993). Teacher use of descriptive analysis data to implement

interventions to decrease student's problem behaviors. *Journal of Applied Behavior Analysis, 26(2),* 227-238.

[39]Levi, D. (2014). *Group dynamics for teams* (4th ed.). Thousand Oaks, CA: Sage Publications, Inc.

[40]Lonnecker, C., Brady, M. P., McPherson R., & Hawkins, J. (1994). Video self-modeling and cooperative classroom behavior in children with learning and behavior problems: Training and generalization effects. *Behavior Disorders, 20,* 24-34.

[41]Luthans, F. (2015). Fred Luthans: The anatomy of a 50-year academic career. *University of Nebraska-Lincoln.* Retrieved on July 26, 2015 from https://www.youtube.com/ watch?v=eVd53xKOi2I.

[42]Luthans, F., & Kreitner, R. (1985). *Organizational behavior modification and beyond,* Glenview, IL: Scott, Foresman and Company.

[43]Luthans, F. (2008). *Organizational behavior* (11th ed.). New York, NY: McGraw-Hill Irwin.

[44]Luthans, F., Luthans, B. C., & Luthans, K. W. (2015). *Organizational behavior: An evidence-based approach* (13th ed.). Charlotte, NC: Information Age Publishing, Inc.

[45]Malik, S. H. (2012). A study of relationship between leader behaviors and subordinate job expectancies: A path-goal approach. *Pakistan Journal of Commerce and Social Sciences*, 6 (2), 357-371.

[46]Morasso, A. (2011). *Follower voice: Influence on leader behavior* (Doctoral dissertation). Retrieved from http://search.proquest.com.une.idm.oclc.org/pqdt/advanced?acco untid=12756.

[47]Moore, J. W., & Fisher, W. W. (2007). The effects of videotape modeling on staff acquisition of functional analysis methodology. *Journal of applied behavior analysis, 40(1)*, 197-202.

[48]Newstrom, J. W. (2011). *Organizational behavior: Human behavior at work,* New York, NY: McGraw-Hill Irwin.

[49]Northouse, P. G. (2013). *Leadership: Theory and practice* (6th ed.), New Delhi, India: Sage Publications.

[50]Odetunde, O. J. (2013). Influence of transformational and transactional leaderships, and leaders' sex on organizational conflict management behaviour. *Gender & Behavior*, 11 (1), 5323-5335.

[51]Owens, B. P., & Hekman, D. R. (2012). Modeling how to grow: An inductive examination of humble leader behaviors, contingencies, and outcomes. *Academy of Management Journal*, 55(4), 787-818.

[52]Peterson, R. S., & Behfar, K. J. (2005). Leadership as group regulation. *The psychology of leadership: New perspectives and research.* Mahwah, NJ: Lawrence Erlbaum Associates, Publishers.

[53]Powell, C. (2012). *It worked for me: In life and leadership.* New York, NY: Harper Perennial.

46

[54]Reicher, S. D., & Haslam, S. A. (2006). Rethinking the psychology of tyranny: The BBC prison study. *British Journal of Social Psychology*, 45, 1-40.

[55]Reid, D. H., O'Kane, N. P., & Macurik, K. M. (2011). Staff training and management. In W. W. Fisher, C. C. Piazza, & H. S. Roane (Eds.), *Handbook of applied behavior analysis* (pp. 281-294). New York, NY: The Guilford Press.

[56]Rice, R. W., & Kastenbaum, D. R. (1983). The contingency model of leadership: Some current issues. *Basic and Applied Social Psychology*, 4 (4), 373-392.

[57]Schriesheim, C. A., Castro, S. L., & Cogliser, C. C. (1999). Leader-member exchange (LMX) research: A comprehensive review of theory, measurement, and data-analytic practices. *Leadership Quarterly*, 10(1), 63-113.

[58]Schriesheim, C. A., Castro, S. L., Zhou, X., & Yammarino, F. J. (2001). The folly of theorizing "A" but testing "B": A selective level-of-analysis review of the field and a detailed leader-member exchange illustration. *The leadership quarterly*, 12, 515-551.

[59]Shields, C., M. (2010). Transformative leadership: Working for equity in diverse contexts. *Educational Administration Quarterly*, 46(4), 558-589.

[60]Skakon, J., Nielsen, K., Borg, V., & Guzman, J. (2010). Are leaders; well-being, behaviors and style associated with the affective well-being of their employees? A systematic review of three decades of research. *Work & Stress*, 24 (2), 107-139.

[61]Skinner, B. F. (1959). Learning and behavior, Carousel Films, Inc., Retrieved on July 26, 2015 from http://www.bing.com/videos/search?q=Skinner%27s+Behaviorism+Theory&Form=VQFRVP#view=detail&mid=10EF15FDE44 6B1476B8610EF15FDE446B1476B86.

[62]Skinner, B. F. (1969). *Contingencies of reinforcement.* New York: NY: Appleton Century Crofts.

[63]Skinner, B. F. (1974). *About behaviorism,* New York, NY: Random House.

[64]Skinner, B. F. (1988). Philosophy of Behaviorism: An informal talk about human behavior and its determinants. Harvard, MA: San Diego State University and Evalyn F. Segal. Retrieved July 26, 2015 from https://www.youtube.com/watch?v=0jgchRbqkJ0.

[65]Stahl, G. K., & DeLugue, M. S. (2014). Antecedents of responsible leader behavior: A research synthesis, conceptual framework, and agenda for future research. *The Academy of Management Perspectives*, 28(3), 235-254.

[66]Stajkovic, A. D., & Luthans, F. (1998). Self-efficacy and work-related performance: A meta-analysis, *Psychological bulletin*, 124 (2), 240-261.

[67]Stevens-Long, J., Schapiro, S., & A., McClintock, C. (2012). Passionate scholars: Transformative learning in doctoral education. *Adult Education Quarterly*, 62(2), 180-198.

[68]Thomas, D. R., Becker, W. C., & Armstrong, M. (1968). Production and elimination of disruptive classroom behavior by

systematically varying teacher's behavior. *Journal of Applied Behavior Analysis, 1(1)*, 35-45.

[69]Touchette, P. E., MacDonald, R. F., & Langer, S. N. (1985). A scatter plot for identifying stimulus control of problem behavior. *Journal of Applied Behavior Analysis, 18(4)*, 343-351.

[70]Vroom, V., H. (1964). *Work and motivation*. New York: Wiley.

[71]Waldman, D. A. (2011). Moving forward with the concept of responsible leadership: Three caveats to guide theory and research. *Journal of Business Ethics*, 98, 75-83.

[72]Wang, L., Hinrichs, K. T., Prieto, L., & Black, J. A. (2010). The effect of followers' behavior on leader efficacy. *Journal of Business and Management*, 16(2), 139-151.

[73]Wegge, J., Shemla, M., & Haslam, S. A. (2014). Leader behavior as a determinant of health at work: Specification and evidence of five key pathways. *German Journal of Research in Human Resource Management*, 28(1-2), 6-23.

[74]White, C. D. (2007). *The leader-member exchange as a function of leader rapport management behavior* (Doctoral dissertation). Retrieved from http://search.proquest.com.une.idm.oclc.org/pqdt/advanced?acco untid=12756.

[75]Yaffe, T., & Kark, R. (2011). Leading by example: The case of OCB. *Journal of Applied Psychology, 4*, 806-826.

[76]Yukl, G. (1999). An evaluation of conceptual weaknesses in transformational and charismatic leadership theories. *Leadership Quarterly,* 10 (2), 285-305.

[77]Yukl, G. (2013). *Leadership In Organizations* (8th ed.). PearsonIN.

3. Evolution of Behavior Theory

Introduction

Many disciplines and theories contribute to the evolution of behavior theory. Though the evolution of behavior theory is slow, much slower than the evolution of the medical field, it is important to understand its beginnings and evolution, through rigorous research, to ensure we do not duplicate research that has already been done and to also understand the framework, in its entirety, for developing a theory of leader behavior.

Evolution of Behavior Theory

Psychology itself is not an old science, especially when compared to the field of human physiology, as an example. The purpose of studying psychology is to answer the question: why do people do what they do? The word 'psyche' is derived from the Greek word soul or mind and 'ology' means 'the scientific study of'. Prior to the formal development of psychology as a science, phenomena, such as the occurrence of behavior, were examined by philosophers.

One of the most prominent and relevant philosophers is ancient Greek philosopher Aristotle, who noted basic rules of association; when two events or stimuli occur enough times together, one, by itself, may generate, as an example, emotion, a mental picture, or response, that the other event or stimulus might do by itself or together with the other stimulus.[4]

French philosopher Rene Descartes stood apart from other philosophers in the early 1600s for noting the influence the environment had on behavior.[4] Descartes did not believe the environment was entirely responsible for behavior; instead, believing that individuals had both voluntary and involuntary control over their own behavior. He also believed all individuals were born with basic ideas, such as a concept of God, and concepts of logic. In the late 1600s, John Locke, a British philosopher and ethicist, disagreed that people were born with these basic ideas and instead articulated that individuals start collecting behavior shaping experiences, from the moment they are born. Thomas Hobbes, another British philosopher, in the late 1600s, also disagreed with Descartes. He believed behavior was a result of either pleasure or avoidance of pain.

While Aristotle seemed to be able to discuss the influence of the environment over behavior in terms of association, Descartes introduced the idea the environment can influence voluntary and involuntary behavior. These ideas had a tremendous influence on Charles Darwin in terms of adaptation and natural selection. Unfortunately, none of the ideas, up to this point in history had been verified through experimental analysis. It is common knowledge, in the field of psychology, that Wilhelm Wundt and William James founded psychology as the scientific study of behavior as it relates to the mind. Wundt published his book, *Principles of Physiological Psychology*, in 1873.

A challenge for the field of psychology, up until the early 1900s, was that scientific study generally focused on the mind and unobservable behavior in conjunction with the environment. Wundt's solution to this dilemma was to identify observable components of consciousness. He established the first psychology laboratory at the University of Leipzig, Germany, in 1879, to train students to observe and measure behavior. Wundt taught students how to use the scientific method, to present stimuli and measure response times, with specifically designed apparatuses. The largest, and most obvious criticism regarding Wundt's study of consciousness, was that it was impossible to interpret experiences in the mind with any sort of accuracy. The study of the mind became known as introspection, and the study of the mind's structures became known as structuralism.

William James, thought to be the first American psychologist, in the early 1800s, did not see the field of psychology the way Wundt did. He was influenced by Charles Darwin's theories on natural selection and adaptation. James believed that psychology should also focus on the function of behavior, relative to the mind, as it occurred in a specific environment. His brand of psychology became known as functionalism.

Shortly after the development of psychology as a field of science, researchers and practitioners started to branch off. One of the most prominent psychologists to evolve out of the early 1900s was Sigmund Freud. He published his book, *A General Introduction to Psychoanalysis* in 1922. Freud focused on neurosis and believed that his patients' problems stemmed from the unconscious, and could be analyzed through dream analysis and free association. Freud is well known today for his terminologies, such as 'Freudian slip', and his model of the mind (id, ego, and super-ego). Though many underlying principles in modern psychotherapy models have derivatives of psychoanalysis, it is probably Freud's case presentations and case studies that strengthened the foundation for meta-analyses of case study research.

While psychology theories continued to evolve from introspection in the early 1900s, in 1913, John Watson, who studied animal behavior for 12 years, published his seminal journal article in *Psychological Review*, titled, Psychology as the Behaviorist Views It, effectively shifting the field of psychology from the study of consciousness to the study of observable behavior.[21] Watson's timing could not have been better; during the time, he published his 1913 article, society's interest in child behavior started to pique. Watson was intrigued by Ivan Pavlov, a Russian physiologist, and his 1901 experiment where he demonstrated that autonomic responses in dogs could be brought under stimulus control. Pavlov's psychology of bringing autonomic responses under stimulus control was called classical conditioning. In 1920, Watson and Rosalie Reynor published a journal article, titled, Conditioned Emotional Reactions, in the *Journal of Experimental Psychology*, where he had replicated

Pavlov's experiment in a toddler, famously named 'Little Albert'.[22] Certainly, by today's research standards, Watson's creation of a fear condition in a child would be unacceptable; however, even though the study left a lot to be desired, it had some very important implications. Watson was able to demonstrate transitive properties of stimuli, when he presented Little Albert with a rat and banged a rod, associating the rat with the painful sound, and then later replacing the rat with a rabbit, without banging the bar, resulting in the same emotional response that Little Albert had with the rat. In essence, Watson and Reynor demonstrated classical conditioning in humans by bringing Little Albert's emotions under stimulus control; and also demonstrated stimulus generalization, which is that the effects of one stimulus can have similar effects as a like stimulus, normally known to be associated with a response, such as in the example of the 'white' rabbit and the 'white' rat.

Edward Thorndike was critical of Watson, even though his own studies supported Watson's findings as far as consequences or reinforcements with predictive properties goes. In 1905, Thorndike published a study where he also demonstrated operant conditioning in animals, though it was not formally recognized as such at the time and demonstrated predictive properties of consequences or reinforcements. He set up what he called puzzle boxes with a reinforcement contingency. Thorndike put a cat in the puzzle box and timed the cat on the time it took the cat to press a lever and leave the box. The cat's behavioral response was shaped by the presentation of a lever and reinforced by the cat being able to exit the box when the lever was pressed. Thorndike may have been the first psychologist to demonstrate a reinforcement contingency, and as a result, he developed what he called the 'Law of Effect'. Thorndike's law basically stated responses that produced a positive result in a specific environment

55

were likely to elicit the same response in the future, in that specific environment, when all variables are held constant; likewise, those responses that produced an aversive result were likely not to occur again when all variables are held constant. Thorndike's experiments were designed to study animal intelligence and instead greatly contributed to behavioral psychology; he continued his studies in psychometrics which helped lay the groundwork for the creation of the Armed Services Vocational Aptitude Battery or ASVAB.

After Watson's 1913 article, he became known as the father of behaviorism. He continued to express extreme views; maintaining that children could be shaped to whatever parents desired and that the study of mental states should not have any consideration in the field of psychology. B.F. Skinner disagreed with Watson and considered mental states to be subject to the principles of behavioral psychology. Skinner referred to thought processes as private events and even though he disagreed with Watson, he did agree that behavioral psychology is the study of observable behavior and that mental states were irrelevant. Skinner did however seem to agree with Watson that humans could be 'shaped' and expanded on Watson's ideas when he wrote a fictional book titled, *The Walden Two*, which articulated how a utopian society could be entirely maintained by reinforcement contingencies. Because both Watson and Skinner held the view that the field of psychology is the science of behavior, and not consciousness, they were labeled as radical behaviorists and sort of ostracized from the field.[1] Behavioral psychologists and researchers today dislike being associated with radical behaviorism; yet, they do acknowledge the major contributions that both Watson and Skinner had to the field.

The most prominent behavioral psychologist and researcher in the field of behavior is Burrhus Frederic Skinner. He was influenced by scientists such as James, Darwin, Watson and Thorndike. Skinner provided operational definitions for processes he saw in previous research. He introduced operant conditioning as behaviors dependent on the environment and expressed the process as a three-term contingency: antecedents, behavior, and consequences. Like Thorndike, Skinner conducted animal experiments, and like Watson could show how the results were relevant to human behavior. Skinner was able to elaborate on the subject of behaviorism in his book published in 1953, titled, *Science and Human Behavior*, ultimately linking the science of behavior to Darwin's 1859 concept of natural selection and adaptation. In *Origin of Species*, Darwin did not state specifically that he believed humans evolved from a common descendant, but he did insinuate it, which later lead to him publishing his book, *The Descent of Man*, in 1871, where he discussed human evolution. In 1981, Skinner published a journal article in *Science*, titled, Selection of consequences, and stated the history of behavior likely started when a molecule came to be and could reproduce itself, and later in the article, stated behavior developed from sets of functions facilitating interaction between an organism and its environment. The point Skinner was making was that humans were an evolving organism, subject to the same principles of behavior that other organisms may be. This was his argument for generalizing his findings from rats and pigeons to human beings.

In the early 1950s, behavioral psychologists and researchers had become dissatisfied with the current scientific journals and their loose standards regarding the scientific method. These scientists met at the annual Eastern Psychological Association meeting, in 1957, to discuss the possibility of developing a journal for publishing peer-reviewed research. It was decided that the journal would be called, *Journal of the*

Experimental Analysis of Behavior, or JEAB. A board of editors was established for the journal on August 8, 1957.[11] The board was made up of several prominent individuals, most of whom have worked at Harvard, including Charles Ferster as the executive editor, Richard Herrnstein, and B. F. Skinner. Shortly after establishing the board of editors, the board realized a need for a journal to publish the applicability of research results. Though there was discussion to include an applied section in JEAB, it never happened. The board recognized the need of an organization to professionally manage publishing journals, specifically the business and editorial end of things, and decided to incorporate the *Society for the Experimental Analysis of Behavior* or SEAB. The organization was established on October 29, 1957, with the JEAB board of editors also serving as the board of the organization.[11] Immediately, JEAB was a successful journal with the first publication occurring in 1958. On September 3, 1967, the board established the *Journal of Applied Behavior Analysis*, with Montrose Wolf as the editor. The purpose of the journal, according to SEAB's website at jeabjaba.org, is, "...publishes research about the application of experimental analysis of behavior to problems of social importance."

After a seminal journal article titled, Some Current Dimensions of Applied Behavior Analysis, published in the *Journal of Applied Behavior Analysis* by Donald Baer, Montrose Wolf and Todd Risley in 1968, giving direction to the field of applied behavior analysis, one of the most prominent theories of leadership, organizational behavior modification, or OB Mod, was developed by Fred Luthans and Robert Kreitner in 1975 and expanded upon in 1985. The Baer et al. article discussed that applied behavior analysis should be used systematically within the field, improve behavior, and show that the application of applied behavior analysis technologies is responsible for the improvement in behavior. The article provided for changes in behavior to be observable and methods to be replicable. Shortly after the article's publication, Aubrey Daniels published his seminal article in the *Journal of Organizational Behavior Management*, in 1977, citing Baer et al.'s direction to the field as direction to the field of organizational behavior management with the caveat that organizational behavior management is useful for managers addressing problems in the organizational setting. The literature shows that organizational behavior management researchers are able to meet the objective outlined by Daniels; however, the literature also shows that they are unable to meet the other objectives as outlined by Baer et al. in 1968.[6]

Organizational behavior modification, or OB Mod, as coined by Fred Luthans, refers to providing positive reinforcement, when an individual's behavior is improved, using current operant and behavioral psychology.[15] Luthans and Kreitner developed OB Mod using Skinnerian psychology.[12,14] The model followed Skinner's antecedent-behavior-consequence, or three-term contingency, expression of behavior, except, in light of Bandura's social learning theory, Tim Davis and Luthans, in 1979, and also Luthans and Kreitner in 1985, changed the expression to include a situational and cognitive component and referred to the cognitive component as 'O' for 'organism' to represent an individual's thoughts or thought process occurring after the antecedent and before the occurrence of behavior. Davis and Luthans, and later, Luthans and Kreitner, developed a linear model to express their Skinnarian three-term contingency model with situational and cognitive components: S-O-B-C (Stimulus, Organism (cognition), Behavior, Consequence).

Social learning theory is a behavioral theory developed by Albert Bandura in the 1960s, who also served on the first board of editors of JABA, with B.F. Skinner. He disagreed with radical behaviorists and believed that cognitive processes were relevant. Bandura's study published with Dorothea Ross and Sheila Ross in 1961 was a hallmark study that catalyzed a mountain of research to be developed on modeling behavior and self-evaluation; the latter often being referred to as self-efficacy.

To discuss behavioral theories of research in the context of cognition is completely contradictory to the direction that Watson, Skinner, and Baer et al., gave the field of applied behavior analysis.[2,3,18,19,20, 21] The Baer et al. articles are still valid today (Baer et al. 1968 updated their article in 1987 and titled it, Some Still-Current Dimensions of Applied Behavior Analysis).[2,3,5,10,16]. In addition, thought processes, even though not observable, follow the same contingency principles in behavior analysis.[9,20] Luthans later abandoned OB Mod model by indicating it was radical; however, he continued to apply behavior analysis principles to his leadership models, such as the use of positive reinforcements in positive organizational behavior or POB, and how it relates to authentic leadership theory, and POB as it relates to the development of psychological capital; a model for staff development, to evaluate human value to an organization, in terms of network size, as an example, that can also be applied within other leadership and management models.[12,13,15]

Summary

The purpose of applied behavior analysis has been to predict and control behavior.[9] The field of applied behavior analysis was meant to be far reaching according to Baer et al., and has been used to treat children with cognitive disabilities, guide behavior change agents such as parents and teachers, and develop appropriate settings in schools, homes, and businesses, as examples.[2,3,6,10,16] Other than research geared toward students and teachers as leaders, applied behavior analysis, has also been used for staff training and management, which are also often addressed by organizational behavior management models.[17] Research on leader behavior has not been addressed, using functional analysis; a systematic analysis of variables and their relationships in the environment, in terms of antecedent, behavior, and consequences, to determine separate effects of each variable on behavior.

Chapter Three References

[1]American Psychological Association. (2007). *APA dictionary of psychology*. Washington, DC: American Psychological Association.

[2]Baer, D. M., Wolf, M. M., & Risley, T. D. (1968). Some current dimensions of applied behavior analysis. *Journal of Applied Behavior Analysis*, 1 (1), 91-97.

[3]Baer, D. M., Wolf, M. M., Risley T. R. (1987). Some still-current dimensions of applied behavior analysis. *Journal of Applied Behavior Analysis*, 20 (4) 313-327.

[4]Domjan, M. (2006). *The principles of learning and behavior* (5th ed.). Belmont, CA: Thomson Wadsworth.

[5]Capell, H. C., Barrio, V. D., & Mababu, R. (2013). Applied psychology: The case of the Baer, Wolf and Risley prescriptions for applied behavior analysis. *Universitas Psychologica*, 13 (5), 1721-1728.

[6]Culig, K. M., Dickinson, A. M., McGee, H. M., & Austin, J. (2005). An objective comparison of applied behavior analysis and organizational management research. *Journal of Organizational Behavior Management*, 25 (1), 35-72.

[7]Daniels, A. C. (1977). Editorial. *Journal of Organizational Behavior Management*, 1 (1), v-vii.

[8]Davis, T. R., & Luthans, F. (1979). Leadership reexamined: A behavioral approach. *Academy of Management Review*, 4(2), 237-248.

[9]Fisher, W. W., Groff, R. A., & Roane, H. S. (2011). Applied behavior analysis: History, philosophy, principles, and basic

methods. In W. W. Fisher, C. C. Piazza, & H. S. Roane (Eds.), *Handbook of applied behavior analysis* (pp. 3-13). New York, NY: The Guilford Press.

[10]Gambrill, E. (2012). Birds of a feather: Applied behavior analysis and quality of life. *Research on Social Work Practice*, 23 (2), 121-140.

[11]Laties, V. G. (1987). Society for the experimental analysis of behavior: The first thirty years (1957-1987). *Journal of the Experimental Analysis of Behavior*, 48 (3), 495-512.

[12]Luthans, F. (2015). Fred Luthans: The anatomy of a 50-year academic career. *University of Nebraska-Lincoln*. Retrieved on July 26, 2015 from https://www.youtube.com/ watch?v=e Vd53xKOi2I.

[13]Luthans, F., & Avolio, B. (2009). The "point" of positive organizational behavior. *Management Department Faculty Publications,* Paper 19.

[14]Luthans, F., & Kreitner, R. (1985). *Organizational behavior modification and beyond,* Glenview, IL: Scott, Foresman and Company.

[15]Luthans, F., Luthans, B. C., & Luthans, K. W. (2015). *Organizational behavior: An evidence-based approach* (13th ed.). Charlotte, NC: Information Age Publishing, Inc.

[16]Poling, A. (2010). Looking to the future: Will behavior analysis survive and prosper? *The Behavior Analyst*, 33 (1), 7-17.

[17]Reid, D. H., O'Kane, N. P., & Macurik, K. M. (2011). Staff training and management. In W. W. Fisher, C. C. Piazza, & H. S.

Roane (Eds.), *Handbook of applied behavior analysis* (pp. 281-294). New York, NY: The Guilford Press.

[18]Skinner, B. F. (1974). *About behaviorism,* New York, NY: Random House.

[19]Skinner, B. F. (1981). Selection by consequences. *Science*, 213, 501-504.

[20]Skinner, B. F. (1988). Philosophy of Behaviorism: An informal talk about human behavior and its determinants. Harvard, MA: San Diego State University and Evalyn F. Segal. Retrieved July 26, 2015 from https://www.youtube.com/watch?v=0jgchRbqkJ0.

[21]Watson, J. B. (1913). Psychology as the behaviorist views it. *Psychological Review*, 20, 158-177.

[22]Watson, J. B. & Rayner, R. (1920). Conditioned emotional reactions. *Journal of Experimental Psychology, 3*(1), 1-14.

4. Contemporary Theory Development

Introduction

The scientific method is a large research model for discovering predictive qualities of some phenomenon. Researchers who conduct studies or develop theories do so by careful analysis of frameworks, variables, validity, and replicability. Often-times, researchers spend a considerable amount of time defining those things where the meaning is thought to be obvious. The purpose of this is to develop an operational definition or a working definition of components that contribute to the theory as a whole.

Defining theory

When teaching, I often define theory as a set of generally accepted principles to explain some phenomenon in a field of study; defining theory itself is like defining 'the'. Sharon Ravitch and Matthew Riggan discussed in their book, *Reason & Rigor*, when viewing theory, there are three domains; the first being more of a causal relationship like a formula; the second domain relates to an individual's interpretation of the questions asked and answers received; and the third domain relates to how individuals are shaped by the outside world; the collective sum of experiences.[10] This would seem to suggest that theories could be classified, though not specifically stated. Ravitch and Riggan reference Vincent Anfara and Norma Mertz's book, *Theoretical Frameworks in Qualitative Research*, and stated, "...sensations, which are then given names (concepts), which are then grouped (constructs), then related to one another (propositions), and finally ordered logically..." to become known as a theory.[3,4]

Theory context

It is important to know the context of theory discussion; as an example, theories in mathematics may have specific outcomes when following a specific set of principles, however, a theory in social sciences might explain the occurrence of some phenomena as a correlational relationship or in terms of probability. This example demonstrates the different meanings theories can have in different contexts. Another example might consider theories of leader behavior, where behavior is the crux of the theory, however, it does not actually focus on behavior in terms of behavioral psychology.

66

Whose theory is it and where does it come from?

Ravitch and Riggan stated, "...theory may posit a formal relationship, refer to a hunch held by the researcher/observer, or reflect a set of beliefs about how the topic itself should be studied".[12]

In the famously referenced 1979 book on research written by Thomas Cook and Donald Campbell, they stated, "It is our inescapable predicament that we cannot prove a theory or other causal proposition",[7] helping explain why results are often described in terms of probability, acceptable assumptions, theories, etc. The American Psychological Association (2007) defines theory as,

"1. A principle or body of interrelated principles that purports to explain or predict a number of interrelated phenomena...2. In the philosophy of science, a set of logically related explanatory hypotheses that are consistent with a body of empirical facts and that may suggest more empirical relationships...3. In general usage, abstract or speculative thought as opposed to practice or reality".[2]

The National Association of Social Workers defines theory as,

"A group of related hypotheses, concepts, and constructs, based on facts and observations, that attempts to explain a particular phenomenon".[6] There seems to be some common definitions among varying sources in social science. Initially, a theory may start out as a 'hunch' or 'sensation', leading the researcher to question. The hunch or sensation is then morphed into concepts and these concepts then become propositions. And, as previously stated, these propositions become the theory. Theories only have value if they relate to the specific field; for example, Pythagorean Theory has little value to social scientists in behavioral studies, however, it has great implications for scientists in engineering. In essence, it is the responsibility of the scientist to evaluate and articulate why a particular theory relates to the specific problem being investigated.

Conceptual framework

There is a multitude of published information on theory and literature reviews related to theory. These published works, in many cases, make the issue of theory convoluted; creating a general state of confusion on exactly what it is. The case for conceptual frameworks is that there needs to be a way to inform research and studies. This is clearly done through a theory or several theories that inform and guide research, with regular literature reviews to guide theory development. In the case of leader behavior theory, the conceptual framework is grounded theory, a framework for theory development, and behavior analysis (which includes behavior philosophy, experimental analysis, and applied behavior analysis).

The study of leader behavior is best described under behavior analysis, often referred to as behavior theory. According to the American Psychological Association, behavior theory is "...the assumption that behavior, including its acquisition, development, and maintenance, can be adequately explained by the principles of learning. Behavior theory attempts to describe the general principles of behavior, often deriving these laws from controlled studies of animals".[1] The APA also defines behaviorism as:

"...an approach to psychology, formulated in 1913 by John B. Watson, based on the study of objective, observable facts rather than subjective, qualitative processes, such as feelings, motives, and consciousness. To make psychology a naturalistic science, Watson proposed to limit it to quantitative events, such as stimulus response relationships, effects of conditioning, physiological processes, and a study of human and animal behavior, all of which can best be investigated through laboratory experiments that yield objective measures under controlled conditions. Historically, behaviorists held that mind was not a proper topic for scientific study since mental events are subjective and not independently verifiable. With its emphasis on activity as an adaptive function, behaviorism is seen as an outgrowth of functionalism".[1,13]

The NASW defines behaviorism as:

"The school of psychology and related sciences established by Ivan Pavlov (1849-1936), J. B. Watson (1878-1958), B. F. Skinner (1904-1990), and others to explain behavior in terms of events (antecedent stimuli) that occur before a behavior and consequences (reinforcing and punishing ones) that occur following behavior. Behaviorism contends that many maladaptive behaviors are, at least in part, acquired through learning

69

processes and can potentially be unlearned. Behaviorism has led to the development of social learning theory and of behavior analysis and therapy as models of practice".[5]

Theoretical Framework

Before a study is started, an idea of a theoretical framework has already been considered by the researcher.[8] Research scientist Francois Desjardins, stated in a YouTube video, that theoretical frameworks are, "…a logically structured representation of the concepts, variables and relationships involved in a scientific study with the purpose of clearly identifying what will be explored, examined, measured or described".[8] Sharan Merriam says in her 2009 book, *Qualitative Research: A Guide to Design and Implementation,* the theoretical framework is, "…the body of literature, [and] the disciplinary orientation that you draw upon to situate your study".[9] Theoretical framework development is the product of research developments that are the domain of study, literature review, and problem development.[8]

Applied behavior analysis is the theoretical framework best suited to research leader behavior. It is the science of behavior that relies on defined principles and systematic research on how variables are responsible for behavioral changes. Applied behavior analysis is a subfield of behavior analysis.

Summary

Theories are developed through organized propositions. They must relate to the area of science that the theory was developed for or is used in. Whose theory is it? It is the

70

responsibility of the researcher to evaluate and articulate why a particular theory relates to the specific problem being investigated. The conceptual framework for leader behavior theory is behavior analysis, which includes behaviorism, experimental behavior analysis, and applied behavior analysis. The theoretical framework, or the framework used to inform research procedures is applied behavior analysis.

Chapter Four References

[1]American Psychological Association. (2007). *APA dictionary of psychology.* Washington, DC: American Psychological Association. P. 111.

[2]American Psychological Association. (2007). *APA dictionary of psychology.* Washington, DC: American Psychological Association. P. 934.

[3]Anfara, V. A., Jr., & Mertz, N. T. (Eds.). (2006). *Theoretical frameworks in qualitative research.* Thousand Oaks, CA: Sage.

[4]Anfara, V. A., Jr., & Mertz, N. T. (Eds.). (2006). *Theoretical frameworks in qualitative research.* Thousand Oaks, CA: Sage. P. 17.

[5]Barker, R. L. (2003). *The social work dictionary,* (5th ed.), Washington, DC: NASW Press. P. 41.

[6]Barker, R. L. (2003). *The social work dictionary,* (5th ed.), Washington, DC: NASW Press. P. 434.

[7]Cook, T. D., & Campbell, D. T. (1979). *Quasi-experimentation: Design and analysis issues for field settings.* New York, NY: Rand-McNally. P. 22.

[8]Desjardins, F. (2010). Theoretical framework [Video file]. Retrieved from http://www.youtube.com/watch?v=Ecnufg QzMjc&feature=youtu.be

[9]Merriam, S. B. (2009). *Qualitative research: A guide to design and implementation.* San Francisco, CA: Jossey-Bass. P. 68.

[10]Ravitch, S. M. & Riggan, M. (2012). *Reason and rigor: How conceptual frameworks guide research.* Thousand Oaks, CA: Sage.

[11]Ravitch, S. M. & Riggan, M. (2012). *Reason and rigor: How conceptual frameworks guide research.* Thousand Oaks, CA: Sage. P. 17.

[12]Ravitch, S. M. & Riggan, M. (2012). *Reason and rigor: How conceptual frameworks guide research.* Thousand Oaks, CA: Sage. P. 20.

[13]Watson, J. B. (1913). Psychology as the behaviorist views it. *Psychological Review*, 20, 158-177.

5. The Case for a Theory of Leader Behavior

Introduction

Leader behavior theory can be explained using common expressions in applied behavior analysis. The expression used is the basic three term contingency, in specific contingency schedules. The contingency was tested on a clinical leader in a behavioral health, in a group setting with supervisees, to measure leader response, in the form of reinforcement, to supervisees' case shares or discussion of client cases, to monitor the quality of treatment provided. Results indicated that leader behavior can be influenced by follower behavior as part of the environment. This

74

chapter provides, explicitly, the theoretical foundation for the function of leader behavior, in scientific terms.

Construction: Foundation

To develop a theory of leader behavior, the framework informing the development needed to be appropriately selected. Because the subject of leader behavior is behavior, it seemed logical to explore already established behavior theories. The science of behavior, behavior analysis, is broken down into three fields:

-**behaviorism** is the philosophy of behavior analysis;
-**experimental analysis** is sometimes thought of as 'rats and pigeons' research, which focuses on the clinically controlled environment to test basic principles of behavior;
-and **applied behavior analysis**, which is the experimental application of behavior analysis principles to solve socially critical issues.[12,24]

The conceptual framework for the development of a theory of behavior is applied behavior analysis, theoretical frameworks being behaviorism and applied behavior analysis. The field of applied behavior analysis demonstrates applied behavior analysis technologies as effective tools to research and manage behavior.[13,28] The technologies of applied behavior analysis have a history of focusing on settings designed for people with developmental disability; research shows that much of applied behavior analysis, outside of developmental disabilities, is simply

75

demonstrating that the principles hold true in other settings.[28] Applied behavior analysis does not have an established area of research exclusive to leadership.[28,32]

Literature shows the field of organizational behavior and organizational behavior modification was derived from applied behavior analysis; however, there are no other theories on leadership within applied behavior analysis. In addition, much of the research in organizational behavior and organizational behavior modification is built on constructs that also include constructs around cognition.[20] The direction given to the field, by many prominent researchers, is to focus exclusively on observable behavior and observable behavior changes.[13]

Countless researchers in the field, have identified several types of reinforcement contingencies and described linear reinforcement schedules, where a stimulus presentation must occur one at a time and others where multiple presentations can occur.[7,8] Notable researchers, Tim R. V. Davis and Fred Luthans, Luthans and Robert Kreitner, and Jon P. Howell, Peter W. Dorfman, and Steven Kerr, discussed leadership behavior in terms of a linear reinforcement contingency.[10,18,21] They remarked that there could be a multitude of contingencies happening at a time, which is consistent with what many other researchers have found in behavior analysis.[7,8]

The Davis and Luthans[10] research, in conjunction with Charles Catania[7] and John O. Cooper, Timothy E. Heron, and William L. Heward[7], etc., help to solidify what a behavior analysis expression of leadership might look like: **f(leader behavior)=S^D→R^1 →S^{R+}. This equation is read as: the function of leader behavior is dependent on operant conditions, also known as contingencies in the environment, where the S^D or discriminative stimulus, is the follower's**

initial behavior or discriminative stimulus alerting reinforcements are available for a response or R^1 (R^1 equals one response) where the reinforcing stimulus presentation is unexpected or S^{+-}, meaning the stimulus relating to the response is either positive or negative reinforcement or positive or negative punishment.

Positive reinforcement is the presentation of a stimulus or stimuli to increase behavior. Negative reinforcement is the removal of a stimulus or stimuli (usually a barrier) to increase behavior. Positive punishment is the presentation of a stimulus or stimuli to decrease behavior. Negative punishment is the removal of a preferred stimulus or stimuli to decrease behavior. This expression does not take into account the leader's first presentation of a stimulus, which could be captured in a follower expression: f(follower behavior)=S^D→R^1 →S^{R+-}, which also becomes part of the environment alerting a follower response. To capture this part of the expression, simple and combination reinforcement schedules, in an ABA research design, can be used to further demonstrate how the expression can be tested.[36] Reinforcement is what happens as organisms act on the environment; most applied behavior analysis research relates to how positive reinforcement is delivered, which has been the focus of research for this theory.[3,6,36]

In the scientific equation representing leader behavior, I did not use the commonly known symbol of S^Δ (S delta) because it indicates the end of the contingency, or extinction; a S^D is used when the discriminative stimulus signals the reinforcement of a behavior within that contingency.[8,14,22] The specific schedule of reinforcement or expression used in this theory is S^D→R^1 →S^{R+-}, where the behavior of followers in group settings, as an example, serve as the discriminative stimulus, alerting the leader that his or her respondent behavior will be reinforced (likewise, the leader behavior may be the discriminative stimulus alerting the followers that their behavior will be reinforced). Given the quality of the stimulus presentation, the leader may present a positive reinforcement him or herself to increase follower participation.[15] The leader's behavior is either reinforced or terminated based on the quality of the reinforcer or continued participation of the followers.[8] If the behavior is reinforced, by subsequent individual responses from the followers, the leader may continue to respond within the reinforcement schedule by staying on subject or stop responding by changing the subject.

The expression can also be extended, by stating $S^D \rightarrow R^3$ $\rightarrow S^{R+-}$, meaning that three responses are required for the delivery of reinforcement, as an example. Though the expression may be used to explain some leader behavior, depending on the operational definitions of responses, the first expression discussed better explains leader behavior in basic terms, especially if the operational definition of responses is anything an organism or leader does before or during the delivery of reinforcement; in the context of leader behavior, the reinforcement might be anything the followers do.

In my ABA design, during doctoral research, where I evaluated leader behavior in a group setting, the baseline condition, phase A, was measured by how much of the time a reinforcement was delivered by the leader, after or during each discriminative stimulus presentation by individuals in the group; in terms of simple schedules, the individuals from the group unknowingly delivered reinforcement, or delivered reinforcement on variable interval. The average of reinforcements, during the baseline phase, phase A, became the baseline variable time or interval. During the intervention condition, phase B, the reinforcements or conversational participation, such as case shares to the clinical leader, were delivered at increased amounts of time or intervals, by individuals in the group, to see if the leader would change his behavior, by him increasing or decreasing the amount of time engaged in the delivery of positive reinforcement. The change in behavior helped to demonstrate the leader behavior expression as an accurate expression that can be used in continued scientific research on leader behavior.

Leader behavior can be more appropriately explained by labeling the three-term contingency expression as a compound schedule of reinforcement accepted in the field; for example, a chained schedule of reinforcement requires the first behavior to occur, as reinforced by the second behavior, with each reinforcing behavior serving as a discriminant stimulus for the next, until the end of the contingency.[7] In a chained reinforcement contingency, the reinforcement is exclusive to the occurrence of a behavior (normally discussed by behaviorists as steps required to make a peanut butter and jelly sandwich; subsequent steps are contingent on the previous step).[8] Unlike a chained reinforcement schedule, a concurrent reinforcement schedule does not require such a sequential presentation of stimuli and means at least two schedules of reinforcement are available simultaneously. A conversation might be a concurrent schedule of reinforcement, where an individual's response may be to engage in conversation or other behaviors. It is possible that components of conversation could be represented by other reinforcement schedules; however, concurrent reinforcement seems to capture leader behavior the best, in most contexts. All other behaviors, not fitting concurrent reinforcement schedules, can be described by other compound schedules of reinforcement accepted in the behavior analysis field, and do not invalidate leader behavior theory as discussed in this text.

Compound schedules are defined by the combination of simple schedules. In terms of leader behavior, the two components, or simple schedules, available simultaneously, are the variable interval (VI) schedule (variable amount of time spent responding) and everything else that is not being studied, but is reinforced, also known as differential reinforcement of other behaviors or DRO. In terms of the concurrent schedule regarding the clinical leader's behavior, in the case study below, when the conversation is complete, after all the responses given at variable intervals, the terminal link in the chain is the last step at the end of the conversation, where the clinical leader engages in other behaviors (DRO). Simple schedules of reinforcement, which make up the components of a compound schedule of reinforcement, are used to describe the delivery of reinforcement more specifically (rate or occurring every unknown number of responses, interval or time that is unknown time, etc., or differential reinforcement delivered based on previous response rate or time). Rates and intervals can be fixed (FR and FI) or variable (VR or VI); variable ratios have the highest response rates.[7,11] The designation of the compound schedule label discusses how the simple schedules function.

The initial variable interval is always unknown and is the baseline; this variable interval or reinforcement average, once identified, serves as the baseline for the single-subject or case design, or phase A of single-subject research designs. The leader behavior, prior to phase B, would be explicitly expressed in applied behavior analysis terms as: Concurrent VR DRO. As previously stated, this is how schedules of reinforcement are typically expressed in applied behavior analysis.[7,22] A real-life example of this contingency might be when the last person in a conversation fails to signal to the other person to continue the conversation and instead is offering reinforcement of another behavior, which may be to end the conversation.

In essence, for this research, I measured changes in a clinical leader's behavior, using a single-case design, where the clinical leader was to engage in a Concurrent VR/VI DRO compound schedule of reinforcement, where his delivery of reinforcements or behavior, was reinforced by continued case shares or discussion by the providers. When the provider's discussion stopped (differential reinforcement of other leader behaviors, or DRO), the clinical leader had to ask a question or make a statement to signal to the followers to start again (discriminative stimuli for the followers); as the followers or providers began to talk (discriminative stimuli for the clinical leader or S^D), the clinical leader made statements and shook his head up and down and back and forth to keep the conversation going (response or R^1). After or during the clinical leader's responses, the providers continued discussion, either positive or negative, to reinforce the leader's behavior (S^{R+-}).

In the case study below, the behavior was measured by how much of the time the clinical leader provided reinforcement in conjunction with provider participation. The independent variable, provider participation, was delivered on an increased VI schedule or stated another way, the independent variable was delivered by the providers, at an increased time above the baseline measure. The expected results were that low levels of participation would increase the delivery of positive reinforcement, and high levels of participation would require less positive reinforcement. Provider participation is an essential part of ensuring that providers understand the treatment they are delivering and for the clinician to ensure the integrity and quality of the treatment being provided.[4,26,27,30]

Case Study

Introduction

During my studies, I established social validity for my research in the context of performance evaluations. In the behavioral health field, as an example, many behavioral health services organizations are required to provide their employees and licensed professionals with performance evaluations per regulation. Some professional licensing boards also expect licensed professionals to receive performance evaluations. The National Association of Social Workers require:

"Standard 3.01 (d). Social workers who provide supervision should evaluate supervisees' performance in a manner that is fair and respectful".[31]

Most evaluations of leaders, managers, supervisors and subordinates rely on the expert opinion of the person appointed over them. It is also common for leadership measures to be focused on the performance of the leader's immediate followers and in the form of survey measures.[35] The best evaluation to predict leader behavior comes from external assessments, specifically observations and from subordinates; evaluations completed by supervisors of managers have been noted as the weakest predictors of leader behavior.

Performance evaluations, whether used to assess previous performance, or future performance, is a probable point of contention, especially when expectations have not been clear. The literature around the use of applied behavior analysis to assess behavior is well documented as being effective in the assessment of behavior and predicting future behavior. In my research design, I used the most common assessment tools to evaluate behavior.

My research was conducted in a behavioral health setting on a psychotherapist leading clinical supervision. Though clinical supervision is multi-faceted, one of the main purposes is for the psychotherapist to evaluate the provider's clinical understanding of the delivery of services as the providers share details about the recipients of services assigned to them. The literature indicated that the providers should be discussing their cases at least 50% of the time in supervision. In this research, I measured changes in the psychotherapist's behavior, using a single-case design, where the clinical leader was engaging in a Concurrent VI DRO compound schedule of reinforcement; providing reinforcements to providers for participation in group clinical supervision. The behavior was measured by how much of the time the clinical leader provided reinforcement in conjunction with provider participation. The independent variable, provider participation, was delivered on an increased VI schedule to evaluate changes in the leader's behavior; the independent variable was delivered by the providers, at an increased rate above baseline. The expected results were that low levels of participation would increase the delivery of positive reinforcement by the clinical leader, and high levels of participation would require less positive reinforcement.

Research Questions

The study investigated the following: (1) How can research methods in applied behavior analysis be used to provide recommendations to improve leader behavior and efficiency in a 501 (c) 3 behavioral health organization? Can an expression informed by applied behavior analysis, to describe leader behavior, be used in scientific research; and (2) How does the leader's behavior change to accomplish group goals; when the delivery schedule of the independent variable such as case shares, is increased, will the leader change his or her behavior to support the group?

Setting

The experiment took place at a Maine-based 501 C 3 non-profit behavioral health organization. The leader's behavior and change in behavior after the introduction of the independent variable, were measured in the group clinical supervision setting, where clinical supervision was regularly provided. The room had the appearance of being a welcoming environment, with furniture that might exist in a common household. The clinical groups are typically three hours in duration and occur one to two times a month. Each clinical session for observation was broken down into one-hour sessions regardless of whether another session immediately followed. Observations took place over a three-month period.

Participants

The clinical leader was selected based off his seniority and willingness to participate in a single case research design. This person was selected because some of his work occurred in a group setting, where he was responsible for provider participation, and providing guidance on the delivery of behavioral health services. The clinical leader can influence the providers; successful group work is based on how well the group interacts. The subordinate providers were selected based off having a commitment to clinical supervision with the clinical leader and their willingness to participate in the research design. All participant rights were protected in accordance with law guiding research with live subjects.

Data Collection and Instrumentation

An ABA single-case research design was the experimental design for my research, where phase A was the baseline phase for the dependent variable, and phase B was the intervention or introduction phase of the independent variable. A scatter plot was used to demonstrate a line of best fit or coefficient to describe the temporal pattern of variables that were the percentage of time the leader delivers positive reinforcement on the y-axis, and the three baseline sessions on the x-axis; which is consistent with common baseline analysis procedures found in applied behavior analysis.[34] During the introduction phase B, I contacted individuals in the group to discuss their delivery of reinforcements on a VI schedule higher than the baseline VI schedule. The second phase A of the design was a follow-up, where the independent variable was withdrawn to ensure observable behavior had returned to baseline.[9,19]

The leader's behavior was the dependent variable, which was measured by his delivery of positive reinforcement. The discriminative stimulus to alert the leader that a reinforcement was available was the provider's beginning participation. When the provider was speaking or finished speaking, the clinician would deliver a reinforcement to increase case shares, or provide a reinforcer for another behavior and terminate the reinforcement schedule. See Figure 5.1 for an Excel graphing table, consistent with tables typically used in applied behavior analysis.[19]

Direct observation and partial interval recording procedures are the most preferred data collection method in applied behavior analysis.[3,8,17,25,34] A continuous 10-second partial

85

interval recording procedure was used to observe behavior as well as behavior occurring during and after the introduction phase B. Each hour was broken down into 60 minutes with every ten seconds of recordable behavior counting as one behavior. Therefore, behavior occurring during the 10 seconds was only counted once (regardless of the response and was counted as one behavior if it was the behavior of interest), and then counted again during the next subsequent 10 seconds if the same behavior was still occurring. The procedure helps to show what percentage of time behavior was taking place during observation. This was calculated by dividing the number of intervals where the behavior occurred by the total number of intervals and multiplying by 100.[33] The taxonomies of behavior that were recorded were antecedents: provider behaviors that are engaging the leader, asking a question, discussing clinically related subjects, and case shares; behaviors: the clinical leader's behaviors that were encouraging more case shares, questions about case shares, directives to continue case shares; consequences: provider behavior occurring after or during the clinical leader's behavior that were engaging the leader, asking a question, and case shares.

The baseline phase, and all subsequent phases, were established by observing three sessions per phase. Three data points are sufficient to establish a trend.[5] Each interval was 10 seconds in length, for each of the 12 sessions, totaling 3,240 ten-second intervals. The total intervals were three sessions for the baseline phase (A) totaling 1,080, three sessions for the introduction phase (B) totaling 1,080, and three sessions for the withdrawal phase (A) totaling 1,080.

Interobserver agreement is the most common procedure in single-case research designs; used to evaluate and ensure reliability.[3,19] During the data collection, I trained another observer to evaluate the occurrence and non-occurrence of

86

behavior by showing a video on how to collect data using continuous partial interval recording procedures. James Moore and Wayne Fisher conducted a study where they successfully trained observers in functional behavior analysis to collect data.[23] Their training consisted of a PowerPoint and video lecture relating to functional behavioral assessments. Moore and Fisher demonstrated that video modeling was efficacious in gaining mastery level assessments from trainees when they assessed actual individuals after a lecture.

Inter-observer agreement was obtained on 67% of the continuous 10s partial interval recording procedures (2,160 intervals of 3,240 intervals). The occurrence agreement among the two observers was calculated (the number of occurrence agreements plus number of non-occurrence agreements, divided by occurrence agreements plus non-occurrence agreements plus occurrence disagreements, rounding down and multiplying by 100); the non-occurrence agreement was also calculated (total non-occurrence agreement, divided by non-occurrence agreement plus the total occurrence disagreement, rounding down and multiplied by 100); and lastly, the total inter-observer agreement was calculated (the total occurrence agreement plus the total non-occurrence agreement, divided by the total occurrence agreement plus the total non-occurrence agreement plus the total occurrence disagreement, rounding down, multiplied by 100)[16,33] (F.C. Mace, templated from personal communication, March 26, 2008).

Methodology and Results

The most senior clinical leader, in an organization where the study took place, agreed to participate in the study. The person regularly provided at least one group supervision for at least three hours each month. For the purposes of this research, each hour

87

counted as one snapshot in time, and was considered a session. The provider participants were providers of adult and children's case management. The group consisted of two case management providers and one case management supervisor. The second date for supervision, the director of developmental services also attended for supervision; it was not anticipated that she would be attending, and therefore she was not part of the intervention phase. It should be noted that the supervisor left the meeting early during the third session of the intervention after 39 minutes. The director of developmental services attended the third date but did not attend the fourth.

Data was collected using 10-second continuous partial interval recording procedures; each hour, or session, was broken down into 10-second intervals, where behavior of interest being positive reinforcement delivered by the group leader in conjunction with case shares, were recorded. Variables of interest were analyzed when they occurred simultaneously, with each variable being counted once if it occurred during an interval, and again each time if it was occurring in subsequent intervals. The group never used identifying information during the meetings; usually only using the first name of clients. The group leader normally held his supervisions in three-hour spans. Data was collected on May 5, 2016 (three-hour supervision), May 24, 2016 (three-hour supervision), June 14, 2016 (two-hour supervision) and July 12, 2016 (three-hour supervision; data was collected on the first hour only, which was the final data collection session). Group supervision was scheduled by the group leader to meet his operational need with individual supervision occurring at various times throughout the month to meet state supervision requirements.

The group leader was informed to run the groups as he normally would. During the groups, he showed videos and had

88

guest speakers. On May 5, 2016, the group was shown a video for 29% of the time. On May 24, 2016, the group leader had a speaker present for 39% of the time. On May 24, 2016, for the intervention phase B, all providers, except for the director of developmental services, were instructed to increase the amount of case shares. Prior to the next session, the second phase A, providers were instructed to participate as they normally would. See Table 5.1 for the variable occurrence percentages. All numbers were rounded to the nearest whole number.

Table 5.1
Variable Occurrence Percentages

	First Session		Second Session		Third Session		
	Number of Intervals Occurred	Percentage of time	Number of Intervals Occurred	Percentage of time	Number of Intervals Occurred	Percentage of time	Totals
Baseline (Phase A)							
Case Shares	239	66%	226	63%	53	15%	48%
Video	0	0%	82	23%	229	63%	29%
Positive Reinforcement	138	38%	126	35%	43	12%	28%
Intervention (Phase B)							
Case Shares	271	75%	87	24%	148	41%	47%
Speaker	0	0%	230	64%	191	53%	39%
Positive Reinforcement	96	27%	36	10%	119	33%	23%
Follow-up (Second Phase A)							
Case Shares	332	92%	319	89%	246	68%	83%
Positive Reinforcement	194	54%	196	54%	140	39%	49%

Inter-observer Agreement

The purpose of inter-observer agreement is to document the occurrence or non-occurrence of behavior in conjunction with another observer to ensure the reliability of the data collected. Inter-observer agreement was obtained on 2,160 of the 3,240 intervals, or 67% of the intervals. The occurrence agreement was 98% (706 occurrence agreements plus 1,428 non-occurrence agreements, divided by 706 occurrence agreements plus 1,428 non-occurrence agreements plus 26 occurrence disagreements, rounding down and multiplying by 100). The non-occurrence agreement was also 98% (1,428 non-occurrence agreement, divided by 1,428 non-occurrence agreement plus 26 occurrence disagreement, rounding down and multiplied by 100). The total inter observer agreement was 99% (706 occurrence agreement plus the total non-occurrence agreement of 2,856, divided by the total occurrence agreement of 706 plus the total non-occurrence agreement of 2,856, plus the total occurrence disagreement of 26, rounding down, multiplied by 100) [16,33] (F.C. Mace, templated from personal communication, March 26, 2008). See Table 5.2 for data.

Table 5.2
Inter-Observer Agreement

| | | Observer One | |
		Agree	Disagree
Observer Two	Agree	706	1,428
	Disagree	1,428	26

Analysis of Research Questions

Research question one. *How can research methods in applied behavior analysis be used to provide recommendations to improve leader behavior and efficiency in a 501 (c) 3 behavioral health organization? Can an expression informed by applied behavior analysis, to describe leader behavior, be used in scientific research?*

An expression describing the reinforcement contingencies related to leader behavior was developed as informed by the literature.[7,22] This expression described what would seem to be bidirectional conversational reinforcement

90

contingency, whereas when the providers change the amount of case shares, the leader's behavior was also effected in the form of his delivery of positive reinforcement. The occurrence of behavior was simultaneous; as the providers shared case information, the leader also provided reinforcement either verbally or with body language. Shaking of the head was the only body language reinforcement recorded. Only reinforcement occurring during the same intervals was counted. A scatterplot analysis and line of best fit using Excel was used to verify that there was a relationship between the delivery of reinforcement and case shares. The expression presented in this book, describing leader behavior, captures the function of leader behavior, especially when discussed in the terms of simple reinforcement schedules.

The average variable ratio (VR) for the baseline phase was 1.63 (total case shares divided by total delivery of positive reinforcement, rounded to the nearest hundredth place). The VR is now expressed as VR 1.63, which is updated to be a variable interval (VI), now that the rate of reinforcement is known. This changes the leader behavior expression, as informed by the literature, to Concurrent VI 1.63 DRO (concurrent: variable interval 1.63, differential reinforcement of all other behaviors), also read as, leader behavior is a function of a concurrent schedule, of two simple schedules combined, with reinforcement being delivered on a variable interval of 1.63, where all other behaviors are not reinforced. In the intervention phase the average VI was 2.02. The follow-up phase, or second phase A, where the independent variable was withdrawn, the average VI was 1.69.

In the literature review, it was shown that case shares should occur in clinical supervision most of the time when focus on case shares is the goal.[29] Table 5.1 shows that case shares occurred 48% of the time during the baseline (Phase A), 47% of the time during the intervention (Phase B), and 49% of the time during the withdrawal phase (second Phase A). The results for research question one show that methods from applied behavior analysis can be used to successfully measure leader behavior.

Research question two. *How does the leader's behavior change to accomplish group goals; when the delivery schedule of the independent variable, such as case shares, is increased, will the leader change his or her behavior to support the group?*

The expected results during the intervention were that the more case shares occurred, the less positive reinforcement was needed by the group leader to keep the group going (this was because most of the time was believed to be used by the supervisees, however, reinforcement to keep the group going was likely provided by other senior members of the group, which was observed, but not studied). The difference in variable interval averages per phase indicates that leader behavior is influenced congruous to the expectation. A comparison of baseline VI averages to intervention VI averages, supports the expectation that leader behavior, in the form of positive reinforcement delivery, does change. The average VI for the baseline phase was 1.63 as compared to the intervention VI average of 2.02. The average VI for the withdrawal phase was 1.69. It should be noted that providers were informed during the intervention phase to simply increase the amount of case shares they normally would; this was done primarily because it did not seem logical to ask providers to share based on the occurrence of positive reinforcement, which may have been difficult for them to track. See Figure 5.3 for presentation of results in single-case research design percentages and Figure 5.4 for presentation of results in in single-case research design variable ratios.

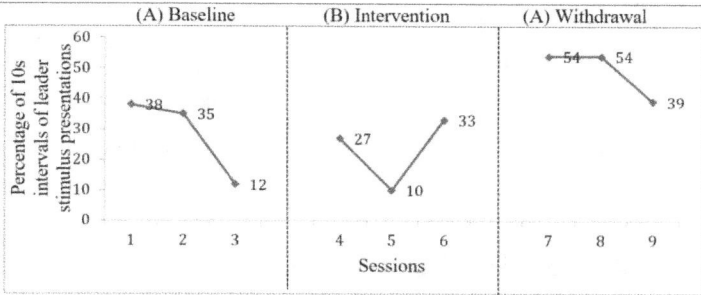

Figure 5.3. Single-case research design percentages.

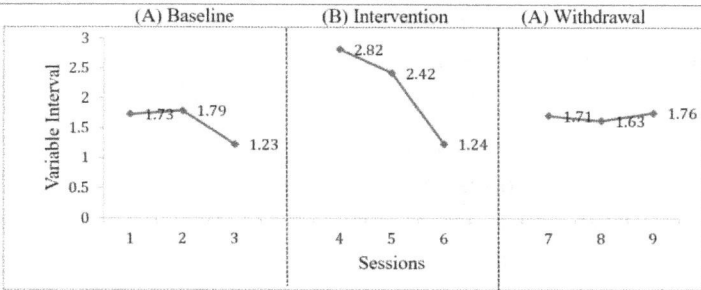

Figure 5.4. Single-case research design variable intervals.

Validity and Reliability

The group leader was selected based on his seniority as a clinical leader within the behavioral health organization. The participants were selected based on their commitment to group supervision. Data was collected on May 5, 2016, May 24, 2016, June 14, 2016 and July 12, 2016, where the clinical leader held group supervision meetings for up to three hours. Each supervision was broken down into one-hour sessions, with each hour broken down for continuous partial interval recording. The results support that methods from applied behavior analysis are

93

effective in evaluating leader behavior (See Figure 5.4) and indicate that leader behavior is effected by follower behavior.[5]

The research discussed in this book is socially valid because it addresses several concerns that society may have[1,13], such as, the development of a theoretical foundation for the function of leader behavior that can be used in scientific studies, a way to measure specific content occurring in group work, and fair evaluation processes such as direct observation.

There were threats to validity that could not be controlled for. Threats to internal validity were noted; on May 24, 2016, during the intervention phase, the director of developmental services attended, which was not anticipated. She was not instructed to increase her time spent on case shares like the other providers were. Additionally, one of the providers left the meeting early during the third session of the intervention after 39 minutes. If both providers were participating in the intervention during all three sessions, the VR/VI may have been higher which would strengthen the case, to support question two, regarding the expectation that leader behavior, in the form of positive reinforcement delivery, does change.

The only threat to external validity noted is that the results regarding research question two may not be generalizable to other like settings because of the threats to internal validity during the intervention phase B. If all variables were held constant through intervention phase B, then the results may be more generalizable. There were not any threats to external validity regarding question one; the leader did provide reinforcement to keep sessions going that resulted in case shares occurring at appropriate levels as indicated by the literature. It is for this reason that I recommend future studies replicate these procedures to establish generalizability.

There were not any threats to construct validity or data evaluation validity. The methods used to evaluate data are strongly supported by applied behavior analysis literature. The scatterplot analysis was included in this research, though not presented here, to verify the relationship between the delivery of positive reinforcement and case shares, as well as ex post facto statistical analysis, mostly to satiate my curiosity and to double-check relationships among the variables. Reliability was established using inter-observer agreement procedures, which verified that the tools used, effectively measured what they purported to measure.

Summary

The purpose of this chapter was to make the case for a theory of leader behavior using principles of applied behavior analysis and to demonstrate how applied behavior analysis technologies can be used to evaluate leader behavior. The research presented follows the scientific model that is commonly used when conducting research.

Chapter Five References

[1]Baer, D. M., Wolf, M. M., & Risley, T. D. (1968). Some current dimensions of applied behavior analysis. *Journal of Applied Behavior Analysis*, 1 (1), 91-97.

[2]Baer, D. M., Wolf, M. M., Risley T. R. (1987). Some still-current dimensions of applied behavior analysis. *Journal of Applied Behavior Analysis*, 20 (4) 313-327.

[3]Beavers, G. A., Iwata, B. A., & Lerman, D. C. (2013). Thirty years of research on the functional analysis of problem behavior. *Journal of Applied Behavior Analysis*, 46 (1), 1-21.

[4]Booth, R. (2014). *Supervision in clinical social work*. St. Marblehead, MA: Center for Clinical Social Work.

[5]Brown-Chidsey, R., & Steege, M. W. (2010). Response to intervention (2nd ed.): Principles and strategies for effective practice. New York, NY: The Guilford Press.

[6]Catania, A. C. (2013a). A natural science of behavior. *Review of General Psychology*, 17 (2), 133-139.

[7]Catania, A. C. (2013b). *Learning* (5th ed.). Cornwall on Hudson,NY: Sloan Publishing, LLC.

[8]Cooper, J. O., Heron, T. E., & Heward, W. L. (2007). *Applied behavior analysis* (2nd ed.). Upper Saddle River, NJ: Pearson Prentice Hall.

[9]Creswell, J. (2012). *Educational research: Planning, conducting, and evaluating quantitative and qualitative research* (4th ed.). Boston, MA: Pearson Education, Inc.

[10]Davis, T. R., & Luthans, F. (1979). Leadership reexamined: A behavioral approach. *Academy of Management Review*, 4(2), 237-248.

[11]Ferster, C. B., & Skinner, B. F. (1957). *Schedules of reinforcement.* New York, NY: Appleton Century Crofts.

[12]Fisher, W. W., Groff, R. A., & Roane, H. S. (2011). Applied behavior analysis: History, philosophy, principles, and basic methods. In W. W. Fisher, C. C. Piazza, & H. S. Roane (Eds.), *Handbook of applied behavior analysis* (pp. 3-13). New York, NY: The Guilford Press.

[13]Gambrill, E. (2012). Birds of a feather: Applied behavior analysis and quality of life. *Research on Social Work Practice*, 23 (2), 121-140.

[14]Gresham, F. M., Watson, T. S., & Skinner, C. H. (2001). Functional behavioral assessment: Principles, procedures, and future directions. *School Psychology Review*, (30) 2, 156-172.

[15]Herrnstein R. J. (1970). On the law of effect. *Journal of Experimental Analysis of Behavior*,13,243–266.

[16]Hoff, K. E., Ervin, R. A., & Friman, P. C. (2005). Refining functional behavioral assessment: Analyzing the separate and combined effects of hypothesized controlling variables during ongoing classroom routines. *School Psychology Review*, 34 (1), 45-57.

[17]Horner, R. H., Carr, E. G., Halle, J., McGee, G., Odom, S., & Wolery, M. (2005). The use of single-subject research to identify evidence-based practice in special education. *Exceptional Children*, 71 (2), 165-179.

[18]Howell, J. P., Dorfman, P. W., & Kerr, S. (1986). Moderator variables in leadership research. *The Academy of Management Review*, 11, 88-102.

[19]Kazdin, A. E., (2011). *Single-case research designs* (2nd ed.). New York, NY: Oxford University Press.

[20]Luthans, F. (2015). Fred Luthans: The anatomy of a 50-year academic career. *University of Nebraska-Lincoln.* Retrieved on July 26, 2015 from https://www.youtube.com/watch?v=eVd53xKOi2I.

[21]Luthans, F., & Kreitner, R. (1985). *Organizational behavior modification and beyond,* Glenview, IL: Scott, Foresman and Company.

[22]Mace, F. C., Pratt, J. L., Zangrillo, A. N., & Steege, M. W. (2011). Schedules of reinforcement. In W. W. Fisher, C. C. Piazza, & H. S. Roane (Eds.), *Handbook of applied behavior analysis* (pp. 55-75). New York, NY: The Guilford Press.

[23]Moore, J. W., & Fisher, W. W. (2007). The effects of videotape modeling on staff acquisition of functional analysis methodology. *Journal of applied behavior analysis, 40(1)*, 197-202.

[24]Morris, E. K. (1991). Deconstructing "technological to a fault". *Journal of Applied Behavior Analysis*, 24(3), 411-416.

[25]Mudford, O. C., Taylor, S. A., & Martin, N. T. (2009). Continuous recording and interobserver agreement algorithms reported in the *Journal of Applied Behavior Analysis* (1995-2005). *Journal of Applied Behavior Analysis*, 42 (1), 165-169.

[26]NASW. (2008). Code of ethics of the National Association of Social Workers. Retrieved on October 14, 2015, from http://www.socialworkers.org/pubs/code/code.asp.

[27]Openshaw, L. (2012). Challenges in clinical supervision. *North American association of Christians in social work.* Retrieved from http://www.nacsw.org/Publications/Proceedings2012/Openshaw LChallengesFINAL.pdf.

[28]Poling, A. (2010). Looking to the future: Will behavior analysis survive and prosper? *The Behavior Analyst*, 33 (1), 7-17.

[29]Powell, D. J. (2004). *Clinical supervision in alcohol and drug abuse counseling* (Rev. ed.). San Francisco, CA: Jossey-Bass.

[30]Reamer, F. (2006). *Ethical standards in social work: A review of the NASW code of ethics* (2nd ed.). Baltimore, MD: NASW.

[31]Reamer, F. (2006). *Ethical standards in social work: A review of the NASW code of ethics* (2nd ed.). Baltimore, MD: NASW. P. 150.

[32]Reid, D. H., O'Kane, N. P., & Macurik, K. M. (2011). Staff training and management. In W. W. Fisher, C. C. Piazza, & H. S. Roane (Eds.), *Handbook of applied behavior analysis* (pp. 281-294). New York, NY: The Guilford Press.

[33]Steege, M. W., & Watson, T. S. (2009). *Conducting school-based functional behavioral Assessments* (2nd ed.). New York, NY: The Guilford Press.

[34]Thompson, R. H., & Borrero, J. C. (2011). Direct observation. In W. W. Fisher, C. C. Piazza, & H. S. Roane (Eds.), *Handbook*

of applied behavior analysis (pp. 191-205). New York, NY: The Guilford Press.

[35]Waldman, D. A. (2011). Moving forward with the concept of responsible leadership: Three caveats to guide theory and research. *Journal of Business Ethics*, 98, 75-83.

[36]White, J. (2016). A functional analysis of leader behavior in a behavioral health setting. *All Theses and Dissertations*. Retrieved from http://dune.une.edu/theses/77/.

6. Analysis

Introduction

The literature and case study discussed in previous chapters demonstrated the fundamentals of evaluating leader behavior within theoretical frameworks. These are the essential tools for describing and evaluating leader behavior. Applied behavior analysis provides already established and well-researched procedures for direct observation and measuring behavior.[8,12,24]

Performance Evaluations

Performance evaluations are the most prominent way to evaluate leaders and subordinates. This process can result in disagreement between the supervisor and the leader being evaluated, which can damage morale and productivity, ultimately leading to the evaluation being invalidated.[3,22] The best practices for evaluations include working with the leader to develop goals that can be observed and measured, and to also include a combination of evaluation procedures such as a survey of subordinates and direct observations.[9,11,19,21,24] Interestingly, leadership literature does not show that quantitative evaluation procedures has been developed for the evaluation of leaders in the behavioral health field. This is likely because the behavioral health field is made up of various providers such as psychologists, psychotherapists, mental health nurse practitioners, social workers, and a multitude of paraprofessionals.[6]

It is important to note direct observation procedures are only a small component of the whole evaluation process; though my research only focused on observations and quantitative data collection procedures, it should be noted that this component is typically missing in evaluation processes. A functional analysis, normally referred to as a functional behavior assessment or FBA, for students in school systems, focuses on:

- records review;
- rating scales;
- interviews;
- observation and data collection;
- and analysis.

102

One possibility would be to follow the FBA format when evaluating personnel performance; for example:

- review the personnel file and mutually agreed upon goals or benchmarks;
- conduct surveys;
- conduct interviews;
- observation and data collection;
- and analyze the data and complete the evaluation

This recommendation parallels best practices for performance evaluations, with the exception that observation and data collection should be on mutually agreed-upon goals of the leader or supervisor and the subordinate leader or supervisor.[11,23] The leader being evaluated should have a clear understanding of the evaluation procedures, provided by the leader or supervisor.

Discussion of Research Questions

The first part of research question one: how can research methods in applied behavior analysis be used to provide recommendations to improve leader behavior and efficiency in a 501 (c) 3 behavioral health organization, was answered by the data collection results. Continuous partial interval recording procedures are common data collection methods in applied behavior analysis, and were used to measure the occurrence of specific variables.[4,8,14,20,26] Case shares, the most common occurring variable in clinical supervision when the focus is on case shares, should be occurring most of the time, with feedback.[19,21] When the goal for supervision was a focus on case shares, the case shares occurred most of the time, when competing

103

variables were considered, as shown by the research results. See Figure 5.1, in the previous chapter, for the percentage comparisons.

The second part of the first research question: can an expression informed by applied behavior analysis, to describe leader behavior, be used in scientific research? was partially verified through the literature review. The expression was also verified through applied behavior analysis research tools normally used to verify like expressions. To answer this part of the research question, and to develop a theoretical basis for the research in my studies, it was necessary to describe the function of leader behavior. Researchers attempted to develop a linear expression of leader behavior, based on Skinner's ABC contingency model that included a cognitive component; however, this expression which was purported to be informed by the behavior analysis field, violated the direction given to the field because cognition is not considered observable behavior.[1,10,15,16,25,27] The research and literature in the field help to show what an expression of leadership might look like. An appropriate description of the function of leadership, as informed by behavior analysis, should look like the following: **f(leader behavior)=S^D→R^1 →$S^{R\ +}$**. This equation is read as: the function of leader behavior is dependent on operant conditions, where the S^D or discriminative stimulus, is the follower's initial behavior or discriminative stimulus alerting reinforcements are available for a response or R^1, where the reinforcing stimulus presentation is unexpected or $S^{R\ +}$, meaning the stimulus relating to the response is either positive or negative reinforcement or positive or negative punishment. This expression does not take into account the leader's first presentation of a stimulus, that could be captured in a follower expression f(follower behavior)=S^D→R^1 →$S^{R\ +}$, which also becomes part of the environment alerting a follower response.

104

The linear expression describes the function of behavior as a single stimulus presentation and reinforcement made available. This is not adequate to describe continuous reinforcement contingencies, some of which may signal the beginning or end of other contingencies.[7] In this text, I described the reinforcement schedule as a compound concurrent reinforcement schedule, though in previous writings, I referred to it as a compound tandem schedule because I believed that leader behavior had to occur as a verbal or other similar reinforcement to the providers to continue with case shares, and terminate or remain silent, in sequence. A concurrent reinforcement schedule is not as restrictive; behaviors and reinforcements more often had the appearance of occurring simultaneously. Verbal and body language looked like head shaking 'yes', and stating 'yes', as an example; leader delivery of reinforcements occurring for case shares and DRO also seemed to occasionally occur simultaneously during case shares. This does not change the reinforcement contingency, as currently stated, because DRO, in the form of silence, cannot occur first.

The simple schedules that make up the compound concurrent schedule were variable ratios (variable intervals once the average variable ratio was known) or VR, known as encouraging behavior for the providers to continue, and differential reinforcement of other behaviors (DRO), or engagement in other behaviors, which was normally the leader remaining silent. The compound concurrent schedule of reinforcement is then expressed as Concurrent VR DRO; however, since the average VR is known, for example, in session one of phase A (see figure 5.4 in the previous chapter), reinforcement of leader behavior was delivered on a Concurrent VI 1.73 DRO schedule of reinforcement, or viewed another way, the leader kept the group conversation going by delivering

105

reinforcement to the providers, on average, every 1.73 intervals that case shares occurred, which was his response to provider reinforcement. During the intervention, where the VI was increased, the leader delivered reinforcement at greater intervals (less reinforcement). In essence, the second part of the research question is answered; an expression informed by applied behavior analysis, to describe leader behavior, can be used in scientific research.

Question two refers to changes in leader behavior; how does the leader's behavior change to accomplish group goals when the delivery schedule of the independent variable such as case shares, is increased, will the leader change his or her behavior to support the group? The change in the VI from the baseline to the intervention seems to indicate that there may be a point whereas if there is an increase in case shares, there may be less delivery of positive reinforcement; however, it cannot be stated for certain that there is an inverse relationship given that the baseline session three and the intervention session six are almost the same. There simply are not enough data points, within the current research design, to conclude that there is an inverse relationship;[5] however, VI comparisons of the baseline to the intervention and to follow-up, point for point, where there are not any other competing variables, shows that the leader does manage the group to accomplish group goals, when there are changes in provider behavior (see figure 5.4 in the previous chapter). It should be noted that the assistant director, who attended the intervention phase and did not participate in the increase in case shares, could have changed the group dynamics enough to affect the VI (see figure 5.4 in the previous chapter). Her participation was not anticipated because she had not attended any previous sessions prior to the intervention. Additionally, the case management supervisor left early during the intervention, session six. If both

106

providers were participating in the intervention during all three sessions, the VR/VI may have been higher for the sixth session. This would be considered a threat to internal validity. The only other threat to validity, needing to be discussed in this chapter, is the threat to external validly. Because of threats to internal validity, the results for question two may not be generalizable to other similar situations; meaning that other group leaders, with a similar number of provider participants in a behavioral health group setting, might not have similar VR/VI delivery of positive reinforcement to manage the group when there is an increase in provider participation. Lack of generalizability is considered a threat to external validity. There were not any threats to external validity regarding question one; the leader did manage the group through delivery of positive reinforcement, and regardless of threats to external validity, in question two, leader behavior did change. It is for this reason that I recommend future studies replicate these procedures to establish generalizability, through meta-analysis.

The research discussed in this text shows that followers and leaders effect each other's behavior. The leader and follower relationship are a bidirectional relationship.[9]

Implications and Limitations

It is not reasonable to believe that an evaluation of leader behavior, in a field setting, would be without unanticipated events. The first unanticipated event encountered during my research was that the group leader showed a video and had a guest speaker; though it is common to use videos and speakers in clinical supervision.[19] Recommendations for obtaining an accurate snapshot of leader behavior, in the behavioral health setting, are for the evaluator to work with the leader to develop specific and observable goals, and to discuss measurement practices.[9,24.]

The second limitation was the unanticipated change in provider attendees. During the intervention, the director of developmental services was required to attend group supervision to make sure she had received all of her clinical supervision hours. Additionally, one of the providers also left earlier than expected, which may have caused the leader to increase positive reinforcement to keep the group going (see figure 5.4, session six, in the previous chapter). It is possible that variations in the number of attendees also effects the leader's behavior. To mitigate these threats to internal validity, it may have been better to only collect data from a single one-hour session, specifically designated for case discussions, on separate days when group supervision is held.

In essence, it is very important for the supervisor to work closely with the leader being evaluated and to understand that leader's intent for group supervision.[9] Supervisors of subordinate leaders should meet regularly with subordinate leaders to go over goals, observation practices, measurement practices, analysis of task accomplishments, and a preliminary review of the evaluation process. This practice should mitigate any grievances over unanticipated evaluation results. Lastly, it should be noted that positive and negative reinforcement of subordinate behavior is the only reinforcement that should be used, as opposed to positive and negative punishment, to change subordinate behavior, for the long term; punishment may be effective for the short term, however, regular deliveries of positive and negative punishment will damage morale, lower productivity, and increase staff turn-over.[24]

Implications for Practice

Direct observation of leader behavior for annual evaluations is clearly part of best practices. The continuous partial interval recording procedure has a long history of being a tool to observe, measure, and collect data on human behavior. Additionally, data can provide evidence that can assist leaders to understand how they respond to their environment and adjust their behavior based off the data.[24] An accurate evaluation is not only crucial to maintaining leader morale and productivity, it is an expectation, and may be a legal requirement, depending on professional and organizational state licensing boards.

Implications for Future Research

Implications, regarding the current and future research, are:

-Replicate the current study with data collection occurring during the first hour of group supervision on separate dates. This will help to reduce threats to internal and external validity.

-Replicate the current study, and encourage research, for a meta-analysis.

-Replicate the current study across settings to expand the use of applied behavior analysis into other fields.

-Replication of these kinds of studies, into other fields, to extend and contribute to the body of knowledge of applied behavior analysis.[1,2,13]

Summary

According to the literature review and research design, the most accurate way to describe leader behavior in testable scientific terms may be as a compound schedule of reinforcement: Concurrent VI DRO; meaning that leaders engage in behavior that is reinforced by their environment. Likewise, follower behavior can be described similarly.

Chapter Six References

[1]Baer, D. M., Wolf, M. M., & Risley, T. D. (1968). Some current dimensions of applied behavior analysis. *Journal of Applied Behavior Analysis*, 1 (1), 91-97.

[2]Baer, D. M., Wolf, M. M., Risley T. R. (1987). Some still-current dimensions of applied behavior analysis. *Journal of Applied Behavior Analysis*, 20 (4) 313-327.

[3]Barankay, I. (2012). Rank incentives. Evidence from a randomized workplace experiment (Working Paper). Retrieved from Wharton School, University of Pennsylvania, website: https://mgmt.wharton.upenn.edu/profile/1303/research.

[4]Beavers, G. A., Iwata, B. A., & Lerman, D. C. (2013). Thirty years of research on the functional analysis of problem behavior. *Journal of Applied Behavior Analysis*, 46 (1), 1-21.

[5]Brown-Chidsey, R., & Steege, M. W. (2010). Response to intervention (2nd ed.): Principles and strategies for effective practice. New York, NY: The Guilford Press.

[6]Carr, E. R., Bhagwat, R., Miller, R., & Ponce, A. N. (2014). Training in mental health recovery and social justice in the public sector. *The Counseling Psychologist*, 42(8), 1108-1135.

[7]Catania, A. C. (2013b). *Learning* (5th ed.). Cornwall on Hudson,NY: Sloan Publishing, LLC.

[8]Cooper, J. O., Heron, T. E., & Heward, W. L. (2007). *Applied behavior analysis* (2nd ed.). Upper Saddle River, NJ: Pearson Prentice Hall.

[9]Daniels, A. C., & Daniels, J. E. (2005). *Measure of a leader.* Atlanta, GA: Performance Management Publications.

[10]Davis, T. R., & Luthans, F. (1979). Leadership reexamined: A behavioral approach. *Academy of Management Review*, 4(2), 237-248.

[11]Derue, S. D., Nahrgang, J. D., Wellman, N., & Humphrey, S. E. (2011). Trait and behavioral theories of leadership: An integration and meta-analytic test of their relative validity. *Personnel Psychology*, 64, 7-52.

[12]Fisher, W. W., Groff, R. A., & Roane, H. S. (2011). Applied behavior analysis: History, philosophy, principles, and basic methods. In W. W. Fisher, C. C. Piazza, & H. S. Roane (Eds.), *Handbook of applied behavior analysis* (pp. 3-13). New York, NY: The Guilford Press.

[13]Gambrill, E. (2012). Birds of a feather: Applied behavior analysis and quality of life. *Research on Social Work Practice*, 23 (2), 121-140.

[14]Horner, R. H., Carr, E. G., Halle, J., McGee, G., Odom, S., & Wolery, M. (2005). The use of single-subject research to identify evidence-based practice in special education. Exceptional Children, 71 (2), 165-179.

[15]Luthans, F. (2015). Fred Luthans: The anatomy of a 50-year academic career. *University of Nebraska-Lincoln*. Retrieved on July 26, 2015 from https://www.youtube.com/ watch?v=eVd53xKOi2I.

[16]Luthans, F., & Kreitner, R. (1985). *Organizational behavior modification and beyond,* Glenview, IL: Scott, Foresman and Company.

[17]Mace, F. C., Pratt, J. L., Zangrillo, A. N., & Steege, M. W. (2011). Schedules of reinforcement. In W. W. Fisher, C. C.

Piazza, & H. S. Roane (Eds.), *Handbook of applied behavior analysis* (pp. 55-75). New York, NY: The Guilford Press.

[18]Maine Department of the Secretary of State. (2016). Retrieved on May 4, 2016, from http://www.maine.gov/sos/cec/rules/10/chaps10.htm#193.

[19]Milne, D. (2009). *Evidence-based clinical supervision.* Malden, MA: Wiley-Blackwell.

[20]Mudford, O. C., Taylor, S. A., & Martin, N. T. (2009). Continuous recording and interobserver agreement   algorithms reported in the *Journal of Applied Behavior Analysis* (1995-2005). *Journal of Applied Behavior Analysis*, 42 (1), 165-169.

[21]Powell, D. J. (2004). *Clinical supervision in alcohol and drug abuse counseling* (Rev. ed.). San Francisco, CA: Jossey-Bass.

[22]Reamer, F. (2006). *Ethical standards in social work: A review of the NASW code of ethics* (2nd ed.). Baltimore, MD: NASW.

[23]Reid, D. H., O'Kane, N. P., & Macurik, K. M. (2011). Staff training and management. In W. W. Fisher, C. C. Piazza, & H. S. Roane (Eds.), *Handbook of applied behavior analysis* (pp. 281-294). New York, NY: The Guilford Press.

[24]Reid, D. H., & Parsons, M. B. (2006). *Supervisory strategies for maximizing work effort and work enjoyment* (2nd ed.)(Vol. 3). Morganton, NC: Habilitative Management Consultants, Inc.

[25]Skinner, B. F. (1974). *About behaviorism,* New York, NY: Random House.

[26]Thompson, R. H., & Borrero, J. C. (2011). Direct observation. In W. W. Fisher, C. C. Piazza, & H. S. Roane (Eds.), *Handbook*

of applied behavior analysis (pp. 191-205). New York, NY: The Guilford Press.

[27]Watson, J. B. (1913). Psychology as the behaviorist views it. *Psychological Review*, 20, 158-177.

7. Motivation

Introduction

As leaders, we often think of motivation as an individual's will to complete some task. In scientific terms, motivation has a specific meaning with a set of principles used to either augment or decrease a drive to complete tasks. Motivation is not simply will or choice, it is referred to as a drive. The concept of motivation was a prominent subject in behavior theory during the early to mid-1900s. The question still remains; how do we get people to do what we want them to do?

Motivation Evolution

The social science field of psychology focuses on why people do what they do. Similarly, motivation is the crux of leadership studies. As leaders, we want to know how to get people to do what we want them to do. Surely, it would seem logical to try to understand why people do what they do to understand how to get people to do what we want them to do. Though these two fields seem similar in scope and research, are we really talking about the same thing?

William James, one of the first American psychologists, also known as the 'Father of American Psychology', proposed in the early 1900s that motivation was a result of survival instincts. Follow-on theorists built upon this idea and indicated that people are born with certain drives, such as the need for food, warmth, safety, etc. It wasn't until 1943 that Abraham Maslow published his theory on the hierarchy of needs, in a paper titled: A theory of human motivation, where he discussed psychological needs ascending from basic needs to more complex needs, up to and including the need for self- actualization.[11] In terms of self-actualization, Maslow stated that once all other needs are met, in each of the five stages, psychological, security, social, self-worth, and finally self-actualization, individuals may be motivated to take up other causes, such as a musician playing music, or a poet writing poetry, if these individuals were going to truly be happy or self-actualized. Additionally, Maslow discussed homeostasis in his paper as the body's natural ability to maintain bodily functions. Deviations from homeostasis is what catalyzes an individual to act to restore a sense of balance; this theory has sometimes been referred to as drive theory. Behaviorist Clark Hull, who was also influenced by Darwin, Pavlov, Watson, and Thorndike, introduced Drive-Reduction Theory in 1943. The theory was based on the concept of homeostasis and the belief that all individuals had biological needs, or drives, that catalyze behavior. Hull referred to these drives as internal states of tension or arousal. He believed that motivation resulted from attempts to reduce tension and achieve a state of homeostasis.[10]

116

The hierarchy of needs theory is partially supported by John Bowlby, who was born to an English family with royal connections. He had very little contact with his mother and father, as was traditional of those who were royalty at the time. Bowlby developed attachment theory and commonly referenced his personal upbringing to demonstrate how the theory is relevant. He emphasized the importance of developing secure attachment, a positive psychological bond between two people, and that it was a matter of survival.[7] Failure to develop the appropriate attachments to parents, specifically the mother, before the age of three, led to symptoms similar to those found in what we would consider today, anti-social personality disorder.

Though Bowlby focused largely on basic needs such as feeding, safety, etc., Harry Harlow elaborated on Bowlby's ideas and conducted an experiment, where he introduced young monkeys to a wire maternal monkey that met the basic need of feeding and another wire maternal monkey that was covered in a soft cloth. He found that it wasn't enough to meet basic needs, and that the monkeys ultimately preferred the wire maternal monkey covered in cloth, which seemed to contradict Bowlby's theory and indicate there are individual differences in attachment quality.[8] These individual differences were demonstrated by Margaret Ainsworth, in what became known as the 'Strange Situation' experiment. Ainsworth created situations where nine to 18-month-old children were placed in eight different situations, where the mother was present to varying time intervals and the mother's responsiveness was also varied, with an adult, unknown to the child, to observe the child's behavior and responses. She found most children were securely attached, whereas the others were not, and concluded, that children used the mother as a base to explore the environment and that the degree of secure attachment and exploratory behavior depended on how responsive the mother was to the child.[1,2,3,4,5,6]

John Watson demonstrated learning by association, in his 1920 'Little Albert' study.[22] When individuals have an unmet need, they may associate relevant stimuli with that need being met; for example, a baby who is feeling uncomfortable, might be soothed by a soft stuffed rabbit. The next time the baby is feeling in need of soothing, the baby might cry for that rabbit and would be satisfied by another similar item.

Watson's learning by association has been corroborated, most likely unintentionally, by Swiss cognitive psychologist, Jean Piaget, in his stage theory of development published in 1953. Piaget discussed accommodation as a mental construct used by children and adults to interpret new, but similar, phenomena. The idea of accommodation is like Watson's generalization of stimuli from one stimulus to another similar one. Piaget also stated that assimilation is the integration of additional information into the schema, again, very similar to Watson's learning through stimulus generalization and association.

Other theorists, such as Robert Yerkes and John Dodson have indicated that arousal levels are what motivates others.[16] Their research showed that simple tasks are performed best when there are elevated levels of arousal, and complex tasks are performed best when there are low levels of arousal. This principle is often referred to as the Yerkes-Dodson law. Yerkes and Dodson recommend that moderate levels of arousal are best to approach. Lev Vygotsky, a Russian psychologist, noted that it was important to understand where the individual was at before assigning tasks, referring to individuals as students in his research, and the probability and quality of task completion was dependent on the quality of guidance or instruction.[21]

Much of the focus of Sigmund Freud's work, in psychoanalysis in the early 1900s, is on instinctual drives of personality development. He theorized personalities were a balance of three components: Id, Ego, and Super Ego. The Id is thought to be the part of the personality that focuses on basic needs; it is the part of the personality that is based on what Freud called the 'pleasure principle', or meeting those needs that feel good. The Ego is the component of the personality that maintains balance between the other components of personality and reality; whereas, the Super-Ego is rule-oriented. Freud believed that neurosis resulted from an imbalance of the Id, Ego and Super Ego, and that it catalyzed maladaptive behavior. Congruous to his theory of personality, Freud also developed a controversial psychosexual stage of development; articulating that children go through five stages of personality development where the focus is on learning to manage psychosexual energy. Failure to move through each stage in a healthy way leads to neurosis or maladaptive behavior in adulthood. Anna Freud was less interested in her father's theory of personality development and focused on and developed motivation as it related to anxiety and defense mechanisms to reduce that anxiety.

Early in his career, Alfred Adler, an ophthalmologist, introduced Organ Inferiority Theory, which basically stated people with physical disabilities have feelings of being inferior and will attempt to compensate for it. After developing the theory, he began attending discussion groups by Sigmund Freud, and became a prominent figure in those groups. Adler regularly vocalized his disagreement with Freud's ideas and broke away from him. He created his own brand of psychology, called Individual Psychology. Adler developed his theory further, calling it the inferiority complex, which is a theory that individuals work to overcome an inherent sense of inferiority. He believed that

119

people behaved according to individual and environmental factors. Adler believed that all people were born with what s/he believed were an inferior body and feelings of inferiority to overcome. There are three components to the inferiority complex that defines personality:

-Compensation-people who experience a disadvantage are motivated to put an end to it and success in compensating for the disadvantage leads to success;

-Resignation-people who experience a disadvantage and accept it, which occurs with most people.

-Over-Compensation-people who overindulge in striving to be successful, which leads to neurosis.

Albert Bandura, who was a product of behaviorism, disagreed with the central philosophy that psychology should be about observable behavior. He believed that drives were mostly a result of cognition as individuals worked toward their goals through self-efficacy.

Motivation in behavioral terms

In 1938, Skinner published his well-known book, *Behavior of Organisms*, where he stated specifically that drives were a function of environmental events and not as completely internal states. Examples he gave were: deprivation, satiation, and aversive stimulation. Skinner noted that behavior resulting from drives can be external and observable. He also named one of the chapters, 'Drive Not a Stimulus'. Skinner continued to reiterate this point in subsequent publications.[19]

Fred Keller and William Schoenfeld elaborated on Skinner's discussion around drives in their famous 1950 book titled, *Principles of Psychology*. Chapter nine of the book, titled 'Motivation', specifically addresses drives and motivation in the context of deprivation, satiation, and aversive stimulation. While offering unnecessary information on the evolution of terminology, Keller and Schoenfeld specifically remark that drives and motives are the same. Keller and Schoenfeld remark, "We feel that unless we know the underlying motives, we shall not be able to deal effectively with ourselves and others in the many important affairs of everyday life".

Keller and Schoenfeld make clear in the chapter that a drive is not a stimulus, and instead are a result of operations, such as deprivation, satiation, and aversive stimulation. They define drive as behavioral in nature and remark that it is, "concurrent changes in the strength of many reflexes". It is not simple enough to identify a drive and then establish an operation, such as deprivation of a stimulus or reinforcer, and expect the drive to be observable; for example, depriving someone of heavy metal music will not establish the drive to listen to heavy metal music. Deprivation of food may establish some portion of the drive to eat; however, there may be a multitude of operations relating to hunger. When a set of operations is established to make the expression of a drive more observable, it is referred to as 'establishing operations' or EO.

It is important to remember that operations establish observable changes in a drive and that the drive is not a response to stimuli. Consider the following example: the heat in a house is shut off in the middle of winter; the operation of heat deprivation is established; individuals in the house become cold and develop a reflexive drive to become warm again; the value of turning on the heat is strengthened; individuals in the house turn on the heat;

121

turning on the heat itself is a response that is reinforced by receiving the heat. Being cold is *not* a discriminative stimulus, however, the mechanism or switch to turn on the heat itself is the discriminative stimulus for the response. In simple terms, the reinforcement contingency discussed in previous chapters, $S^D \rightarrow R^1 \rightarrow S^{R +-}$ is the three-term contingency for antecedent, response and reinforcement; now imagine a four-term contingency, $EO \rightarrow S^D \rightarrow R^1 \rightarrow S^{R +-}$.

The term, 'establishing operations' was first introduced by Keller and Schoenfeld and later elaborated on by Jack Michael in several of his papers.[12,13,14,15] He referred to all the operations as motivating operations, with terminology specifically describing how operations change the effectiveness of stimuli in the environment. Motivating operations can be unconditioned (unlearned) or conditioned (learned). An example of an unconditioned motivating operation, UMO, would be food deprivation; we as humans do not need to learn to eat food to become satiated; becoming full abolishes food as a reinforcer. Likewise, a conditioned motivating operation, CMO, is learned; as an example, an individual is served a meal without the proper utensils to eat the food and responds to the waiter to bring the proper utensils, increasing the value, and receives them as a reinforcer to the response.[15]

Skinner noted, in his 1938 book, that the next step for the study of motivation was to quantify relationships regarding motivation. The quantification of the strength of relationships occurred in the late 1950s and 1960s using rat studies and simple schedules. Since that time, motivation, though an important subject, has not been as prominent in applied behavior analysis as operant conditioning. Skinner often referred to motivation as antecedents to responses and did not seem to really accept much of the terminology that other researchers assigned to specific components of operations, though he did use the term motivative operations in lieu of establishing operations. After the publication of Keller and Schoenfeld's 1950 book, studies have become increasingly complex and valuable; however, further discussion of them exceed the scope of this book.

Summary

Drives are often private events, though the behavior resulting from them is often observable. Even though Skinner was clear that motivation is not a stimulus, he did indicate that it was an antecedent to behavior (I would further remark that a drive is the antecedent to the antecedent of the three-term contingency). Skinner and subsequent researchers noted that motivation is reflexive and a product of multiple operations, and that the operations themselves either strengthened or weakened the value of reinforcers in the environment.

Chapter Seven References

[1]Ainsworth, M. D. (1964). Patterns of attachment behavior shown by the infant in interaction with his mother. *Merrill-Palmer Quarterly of Behavior and Development*, 51-58.

[2]Ainsworth, M. D. S. (1967). *Infancy in Uganda: Infancy in Uganda: Infant care and the growth of love*. Baltimore, MD: Johns Hopkins Press.

[3]Ainsworth, M. D. S., & Bell, S. M. (1970). Attachment, exploration, and separation: Illustrated by the behavior of one-year-olds in a strange situation. *Child Development, 41*, 49-67.

[4]Ainsworth, M. D. S., Bell, S. M., & Stayton, D. J. (1971). Individual differences in strange-situation behavior of one-year-olds. In H. R. Schaffer (Ed.), The origins of human social relations. London and New York: Academic Press. 17-58.

[5]Ainsworth, M. D. S., Blehar, M. C., Waters, E., & Wall, S. (1978). *Patterns of attachment: A psychological study of the strange situation*. Hillsdale, NJ: Erlbaum.

[6]Ainsworth, M. D. S., & Wittig, B. A. (1969). Attachment and exploratory behavior of one-year-olds in a strange situation. In B. M. Foss(Ed.), *Determinants of infant behavior, 4*, 111-136, London: Methuen.

[7]Bowlby, J. (1951). Maternal Care and Mental Health, World Health Organization.

[8]Harlow, H. (1958). The nature of love. *American Psychologist, 13:* 673–685.

[9]Keller, F. S., & Schoenfeld, W. N. (1950). *Principles of psychology*. New York, NY: Appleton-Century-Croft, Inc.

[10]Kleinman, P. (2012). *Psych 101: Psychology Facts, Basics, Statistics, Tests, and More!* Avon, MA: Simon & Schuster, Inc.

[11]Maslow, A. H. (1943). A theory of human motivation. *Psychological Review, 50,* 370-396.

[12]Michael, J. (1984). Verbal behavior. *Journal of the Experimental Analysis of Behavior, 42,* 363-376.

[13]Michael, J. (1993). Establishing operations. *The Behavior Analyst, 16,* 191-206.

[14]Michael, J. (2000). Implications and refinements of the establishing operation concept. *Journal of Applied Behavior Analysis, 33,* 401-410.

[15]Michael, J. (2007). Motivating operations. In J. O. Cooper, T. E. Heron, W. L. Heward (Eds.). *Applied behavior analysis* (2nd ed.). 374-391. Upper Saddle River, NJ: Merrill Prentice Hall.

[16]OpenStax College. (2014). *Psychology.* Houston, TX: OpenStax CNX.

[17]Piaget, J. (1953). *The origin of intelligence in the child.* New Fetter Lane, New York: Routledge & Kegan Paul.

[18]Santrock, J (2004). A Topical Approach to Life-Span Development. Chapter 6 Cognitive Development Approaches (200 – 225). New York, NY: McGraw-Hill.

[19]Sundberg, M. L. (2013). Thirty points about motivation from Skinner's book Verbal Behavior. *Analysis of Verbal Behavior, 29,* 13-40.

[20]Sundberg, M. L., & Michael, J. (2001). The benefits of Skinner's analysis of verbal behavior for children with autism. *Behavior Modification, 25,* 698-724.

[21]Vygotsky, L. (1934). Thought and language. Cambridge, MA: MIT Press.

[22]Watson, J. B. (1913). Psychology as the behaviorist views it. *Psychological Review*, 20, 158-177.

8. Leader Behavior Theory

Introduction

Leader behavior theory encompasses three main components: classical conditioning, operant conditioning, and adaptation. In this chapter, LBT and its components are discussed. The environment is the overarching theme of LBT; leaders who engage scientific literature regularly to evaluate and manage their environments, are the most effective in managing their behavior and the behavior of subordinates.

Leader Behavior Theory

The crux of leader behavior theory encompasses all that is part of behavior theory. Its specific focus is on the environment relative to behavior and is always based on what is observable. In each environment, where the leader is influenced or will want to influence behavior, the following three things must always be considered:

1. Association (classical conditioning/various stimuli sharing the same properties)
2. Antecedents, Behaviors, and Consequences (operant conditioning)
>   a. Antecedents alert an individual that there is a reinforcer available
>   b. Behaviors occur because of interaction with the environment
>   c. Consequences, either positive or negative, maintain behavior
3. Adaptation (motivation/drives/arousal/history in terms of deprivation, satiation, aversive stimulation, genetics, natural selection, etc.)

Throughout the rest of the text, these three components will be referred to as Leader Behavior Theory Triple A, or LBT-3 (or LBT-1A, referring to association, or classical conditioning; LBT-2A referring to antecedents, or operant conditioning, and; LBT-3A, referring to adaptation, or motivation, drives, etc).

The development of LBT was meant to fill in the gaps where there was missing information in leadership studies, particularly around leader behavior. It is meant to draw the leader's attention to personal behavior and to the behavior of followers, using a simple ABC method of evaluation with a focus on the environment.

To further demonstrate the role of the environment, consider telling a young child to change their behavior, 'stop falling out of your seat while you are reading [in reading class]'. Will the child stop because s/he was told to stop? Probably not.

Research shows, as previously discussed, that the child may be attempting to fall out of his or her seat to escape from academic demands. Research also shows the child may be falling out of his or her seat because of attention-maintained behavior.[8] It could be that the child does not have any choices in reading, and that a choice might be sufficient to change behavior, as research has also shown.[1,2,7] A functional analysis, using the research tools discussed in the Case Study and in behavior analysis, will reveal the relationship between the behavior and variables existing in the environment.

The research methods for measuring child behavior are well established. They are not well established for the workplace; however, let's consider how the above example might play out in the workplace. It is not always enough to tell an employee to do their work. Imagine an employee who is consistently late with their progress notes; forcing the agency to miss its billing deadline. After telling them the notes need to be in on Mondays by 12 pm, it is found that they are still consistently late by two days. The typical response is to give a verbal warning or a write-up, which serves as positive punishment (presentation of an aversive stimulus to decrease non-compliant behavior). Even though the warning/write-up is part of the environment, it is discussed with the employee with a focus on their behavior directly, letting them know that if their behavior does not change, more bad things could happen per policy. As a leader, we may start to work through the scientific method with an applied behavior analysis framework. The following are the steps we might take:

1. We observe the employee is not getting their notes in on time and want to know why.

2. We review the employee record and find that they have no other outstanding issues. We review the literature on work performance and decide to conduct a time study.

3. We conduct observations of the employee behavior and note that when they are in the office, they are completing their notes. We also check the timestamps in our databases and note that they are submitting notes regularly but are late. It is noted, during a partial interval recording procedure that 10% of their time in the office, on Monday mornings, is spent on client phone calls and five percent is spent chatting with other coworkers. We decide to conduct the observation over a period of at least three weeks because we need at least three data points to articulate a trend. We decide to conduct an experiment/intervention, an ABABC design, where:

a. A is the baseline assessment.
b. B is the intervention that includes the supervisor advising the employee to shut off the work phone while working in the office.
c. A is the withdrawal of the intervention, and the baseline assessed again for a return to base line.
d. BC is the intervention that includes the supervisor advising the employee to shut off the work phone while working in the office and to relocate to another space absent of other employees.

4. After conducting the experiment, we organize the results, possibly into a graph, and find that notes were able to be submitted on time when the phone was shut off, but

that the notes were slightly late when access to coworkers was removed. Though we could conjecture that limiting access to coworkers might be limiting knowledge sharing or influence on morale, we are not really concerned about it because our overall goal was to increase productivity by using information, we know to be true, as evidenced by the experimental design.

5. Finally, we can publish our findings to the employee (even though they were included in the process and consented), and change the environment by limiting phone access during paperwork periods in the office.

Operant conditioning is the contingency leaders will use most in the workplace. Adaptation/drives and association might be more difficult to assess and act on because many of the variables occurring with behavior are present outside of the workplace also. Positive reinforcement is the most effective behavior-changing strategy and should be used whenever possible. In the example above, I used negative reinforcement (removal of barriers to increase compliant behavior), and then once the notes were in on time, I would provide positive reinforcement and fade or thin the need for the supervisor to tell the employee to shut her phone off, so that s/he could *learn* to manage her time on her own.[1,3]

Prominent Issues in the Workplace

A hasty Google search of what employees look for in the workplace will reveal that the environment is the most important. When I typed into the Google search engine, at the time of this writing, 'What do employees look for in a workplace?', several

131

links came up that showed the work environment was the most important variable. Many articles focused on respect, career path and professional growth, and leadership. These variables seem to speak to reinforcement. Though some articles stated that the salary was most important, it was rare. Let's take a look at some of the themes:

Money

So...why is money not the most important? The answer to this could be explained in terms of LBT-3A, adaptation or motivation. Once an individual has accepted a salary, their basic needs (food, shelter, safety, etc.), related to finances may have been met; they are satiated. Though this is not true for everyone, it is true for enough people that we might consider the 'bonus seeker' an outlier. Over the years, as a business executive, I have repeatedly offered bonuses with very little success. So...while money is an important consideration, it is not important enough to increase productivity or keep someone at a job.[6]

Respect and Acceptance

An environment where every employee is treated with respect and acceptance for who they are can be the most important variable in attracting and retaining employees. Respect and acceptance are about positive recognition and positive feedback. While respect is likely more about constant positive reinforcement, LBT-2A, operant conditioning, acceptance is more about LBT-1A, association. Most of leadership and employees want to associate with those who have similar values; sometimes referred to as 'in-group' or 'organizational citizenship'.[9] To build this environment, an organization could publish a mission

132

statement that would represent what the employees do, publish values, publish newsletters, associate with other like prominent and well-known organizations. Employees may be looking for respect both at the workplace, and among their community; a good, strong, positive organization reputation is important.

Career Path

While some employees simply want to hold a job, others are looking for a career path to some end goal. Surely, path-goal theory could be applied to meet this employee requirement; however, we are still talking about behavior, and the LBT-3 component that primarily addresses this concern is LBT-2A, operant conditioning. A career path might be explained by looking at forward chaining.[4] Each step along the way, on a career path, should reinforce the completion of the previous step until the final goal is met. As an example, a behavioral health employer might help its employees become substance use counselors by assisting them with obtaining basic certifications, on company time, leading to licensure as a clinical counseling supervisor (employees must test to become a certified counselor, work on hours to be able to test to become an independently licensed alcohol and drug counselor, and finally, work on hours and attend training to become a clinical counseling supervisor). Each time a goal is met, the organization publishes the accomplishment with positive reinforcement, to the entire organization, through mass email, or the organizational newsletter, as an example, and continues to provide positive reinforcement every step of the way.

Leadership

Employees look to leaders they can identify with.[5] Leaders who can define the environment without ambiguity and maintain appropriate reinforcement contingencies will be the most successful in recruiting and maintaining a workforce. While LBT-3 seems like a straightforward leadership model and can be used with little research and remarkable success, a great leader will constantly associate with prominent leaders that subordinates might look up to, review literature, case studies, books of successful leaders, and attend training, to be able to manage the environment. Leaders constantly engage in self-assessment to hone leadership skills.

Behavior as a Function (point proven)

If I were to ask you what color this text was, and you were to say 'black', I would say that your response is a function of my stimulus presentation which was, 'what color is this text?' Your relationship with the environment is what likely shaped your response. Likewise, if I were to ask you what color this text was and you stated 'orange', then I would need to look at what your behavior is a function of; what is it in the environment that has led you to respond with 'orange' when asked the question? Expand this discussion to leader behavior; what is the leader's relationship with the environment...what is the function of their behavior?

Summary

The purpose of this chapter was to discuss briefly what leader behavior theory is and provide some examples of how it might be applied. Leader behavior theory focuses on the environment with consideration of three components: association of like stimuli and classical conditioning, the ABCs of behavior also known as operant conditioning, and adaptation. Operant conditioning is the most common contingency that leaders will observe and engage in as they lead organizations. **Leaders who engage scientific literature regularly will be the most effective organizational leader.**

Chapter Eight References

[1]Cooper, J. O., Heron, T. E., & Heward, W. L. (2007). *Applied behavior analysis*, (2nd ed.). Upper Saddle River, NJ: Pearson Education, Inc.

[2]Fisher, W. W., Thompson, R. H., Piazza C. C., Crosland K. & Gotjen D. (1997). On the relative reinforcing effects of choice and differential consequences. *Journal of applied behavior analysis, 0(3)*, 423-438.

[3]Hanley, G. P., Iwata, B. A., & Thompson, R. H. (2001). Reinforcement schedule thinning following treatment with functional communication training. *Journal of Applied Behavior Analysis, 34,* 17–38.

[4]Hagopian, L. P., Toole, L. M., Long, E. S., Bowman, L. G., & Lieving, G. A. (2004). A comparison of dense-to-lean and fixed lean schedules of alternative reinforcement and extinction. *Journal of Applied Behavior Analysis, 37,*323-337.

[5]Haslam, S. A., Reicher, S. D., & Platow, M. P. (2011). *The new psychology of leadership: Identity, influence, and power.* New York, NY: Psychology Press.

[6]Luthans, F., Luthans, B. C., & Luthans, K. W. (2015). *Organizational behavior: An evidence-based approach* (13th ed.). Charlotte, NC: Information Age Publishing, Inc.

[7]Tiger, J. H., Hanley, G. P., & Hernandez, E. (2006). An evaluation of the value of choice with preschool children. *Journal of applied behavior analysis, 39(1)*, 1-16.

[8]Touchette, P. E., MacDonald, R. F., & Langer, S. N. (1985). A scatter plot for identifying stimulus control of problem behavior. *Journal of Applied Behavior Analysis, 18(4),* 343-351.

[9]Yaffe, T., & Kark, R. (2011). Leading by example: The case of OCB. *Journal of Applied Psychology*, 4, 806-826.

Leader Glossary

Accommodation-Generalization of a schema to explain another unfamiliar scenario; a cognitive process by which developing children learn to understand phenomena using what they already know.

Applied Behavior Analysis-A science of behavior that relies on defined principles and systematic research on how variables are responsible for behavioral changes (Catania, 2013b; Cooper et al., 2007; Kazdin, 2011); it is the subfield of behavior analysis that focuses applicability.

Assimilation-Integration of additional information into an existing schema; a cognitive process by which developing children learn to delineate between two similar objects.

Attachment-Is the bond between two people, usually the mother and a child.

Attachment Theory-A theory that describes adaptation to environments based on the strength of attachment to others.

Behavior-Is the activity of a living organism (Daniels & Daniels, 2005).

Behavior Analysis-The science of behavior that relies solely on methodologies for observing behavior; applied behavior analysis is a subfield of behavior analysis (Fisher et al., 2011).

Behaviorism-Is the subfield of behavior analysis and is the philosophy of the field.

Classical Conditioning-The transferring of stimuli properties, where a response that was elicited by a stimulus, by itself, is elicited by a second stimulus, after being repeatedly paired with the first stimulus. This brand of behavioral psychology was brought forward by Ivan Pavlov, a Russian physiologist, and his 1901 experiment where he demonstrated that autonomic responses in dogs could be brought under stimulus control.

Contingency Theory of Leadership-Is a theory of personality that is predictive of leader effectiveness.

Experimental Analysis-Is the subfield that is the research component of the field.

Functional Analysis-A systematic analysis of variables and their relationships in the environment, in terms of antecedent, behavior, and consequences, to determine separate effects of each variable on behavior (Catania, 2013b; Cooper et al, 2007).

Matching Law-States that for a behavior to occur, and keep occurring, the amount of reinforcement must be commensurate to the behavior.

Operational Definitions-Definitions of terminology used within a process or research to provide all participants with a common understanding of terms.

Organizational Citizenship Behavior-A leadership theory that considers the leader's relationship with 'in-groups' and 'out-groups' within an organization.

Organizational Behavior Management or OBM-Is an organization management style that uses applied behavior analysis to improve performance (Daniels, 1977; Reid et al., 2011).

Organizational Behavior Modification or O.B. Mod.- The application of behavioristic, social learning, and cognitive theories and evidence based principles to manage individuals in organizational settings (Luthans, Luthans, & Luthans, 2015).

Path-goal Theory-Developed to assist leaders in helping followers to identify behaviors that lead to goals, while maintaining consideration of follower needs, situation, and environment to ensure success and satisfaction of the follower (Northouse, 2013).

Psychology-The field of study that investigates why people do what they do.

Radical Behaviorist-A behaviorist who believes that mental processes is irrelevant in behavior theory (APA, 2007).

Research-Rigorous systematic review of all available materials for on a single subject area.

Research Method-(See scientific method).

Scientific Method-Commonly referred to as 'science', 'scientific method', and 'research method', and refers to five components: 1. an observation or question; 2. literature review (which is ongoing throughout the process); 3. experiment 4. results and analysis; 5. publish and make recommendations. Note: Some texts may list the methodology in a longer sequence; each component has been written about extensively and exclusively.

Self-Efficacy-Is being able to reflect on the self, in some way, to change behavior (American Psychological Association, 2007).

Self-regulation Theory-A theory that states tension in groups is what makes groups function.

Situational Leadership Theory-Focuses on leader effectiveness based on leader styles and situations.

Social Justice-A principle that focuses on values such as responsibility, ethos, freedom, equality, empowerment, and justice or fairness (Carr et al., 2012; Greene, 1993).

Social Learning Theory-A theory that uses principles of cognitive and behavioral theories to explain behavior as a result of observing others.

Supervision-1. surveillance of subordinate effectiveness (Weld, 2012), 2. and, in a clinical framework, through evaluation of case shares (Joubert et al., 2013; Pack, 2015; Powell, 2004).

Target Behavior-Is the behavior of interest.

Theory-A generally accepted set of principles and/or ideas.

Trait Theory of Leadership-Is a theory that leaders have innate abilities to lead; early literature referred to this theory as the 'great man' theory.

Transformative Learning-Learning new models and skills through leader trainings, seminars, and courses.

Transformational Leadership-A leadership theory that focuses on transforming others to perform higher than expected; it considers variables such as emotions, values, ethics, leader vision, and the dyadic relationship between leaders and followers (Northouse, 2013).

About the Author

Jason White is well known for his work in several prestigious roles, to include platoon leader in a combat theater, company commander, mid-level manager in state government, chief executive officer of a large multi-million-dollar non-profit organization, gubernatorial appointee, pro tem., and later elected, board chair of a statewide government school system. Today, Dr. White serves as faculty in the Department of Social and Behavioral Sciences at the University of Southern Maine, and as president of his research firm, PREP Group, LLC. When not actively engaged in research, Jason can be found on the beautiful coast of Maine, with his wife, and beach bum children.

Send correspondence to:
jwhite@prepgroup.info.